CONCILIUM

concilium

1990/6

1492–1992
THE VOICE OF THE VICTIMS

Edited by

Leonardo Boff and
Virgil Elizondo

SCM Press · London

Trinity Press International · Philadelphia

December 1990

ISBN: 0 334 03005 6
ISSN: 0010–5236

Typeset at The Spartan Press Ltd, Lymington, Hants
Printed by Dotesios Printers Ltd, Trowbridge, Wilts

Concilium: Published February, April, June, August, October, December.

For the best and promptest service, new subscribers should apply as follows:
    US and Canadian subscribers:
Trinity Press International, 3725 Chestnut Street, Philadelphia PA 19104
Fax: 215–387–8805
    UK and other subscribers:
SCM Press, 26–30 Tottenham Road, London N1 4BZ
Fax: 071–249 3776
Existing subscribers should direct any queries about their subscriptions as above.

Subscription rates are as follows:
United States and Canada: US $59.95
United Kingdom, Europe, the rest of the world (surface): £34.95
Airmail to countries outside Europe: £44.95

Further copies of this issue and copies of most back issues of *Concilium* are available at $12.95 (US and Canada)/£6.95 rest of the world.

Contents

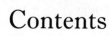

Editorial

The Voices of the Victims: Who will Listen to Them?

12 October 1492 was the beginning of a long and bloody Good Friday for Latin America and the Caribbean. It is still Good Friday, and there is no sign of Easter Day. The dominant accounts were written from the ships which came to conquer and not by the victims waiting on the shore who suffered the effects of the domination. The victims cry out, and their suffering challenges us. This whole issue of *Concilium* will try to be faithful to these protests.

In the first place they denounce the historical and social *injustice* of the process of colonization and Christianization. They condemn the devastation brought about by the colonizers: 'Alas, we were saddened because they came. They came to make our flowers wither so that only their flower might live,' wrote the Maya prophet in *Chilam Balam de Chumayel*. And he continues, with more charges against the Christians: 'Sadness was brought among us, Christianity was brought among us. This was the beginning of our distress, the beginning of our slavery.' The invasion represented the biggest genocide in human history. The destruction affected around 90% of the population. Of the 22 million Aztecs in 1519 when Hernán Cortez entered Mexico there were only a million left in 1600. The survivors are crucified peoples, enduring worse abuses than the Jews in Egypt and Babylon and the Christians under the Roman emperors, as was said many times by bishops who defended the Indians. Today this process continues in the two-thirds who suffer hunger, the submerging of our cities by shanty-towns, ecological aggression, in which the poor and the indigenous peoples are those most threatened with extermination; in the foreign debt, which represents the new tribute which countries kept in underdevelopment have to pay to their old and new masters.

Until the Last Judgment the victims will have the right to protest against the injustice which the Christians inflicted on them: in the words of a sixteenth-century indigenous writer, they were 'the Antichrist on earth, the tiger of the peoples, sucking the Indians dry'. Unless we remove this injustice, we shall never reach the truth of these enslaved cultures. St Paul teaches us rightly that truth is imprisoned by injustice (cf. Rom. 1.18). How long will this truth be kept a prisoner?

Secondly, the victims demand *recognition*. The Indians and the blacks were never really recognized as others, different and equal in status in their culture and religion. They were thought of as animals and treated as such. The first letter written by a pope to Latin America, Paul III's bull *Sublimis Deus* of 1537, sought to establish that the Indians were 'true human beings . . . who should not be deprived of their liberty or of control of their property, nor should they be reduced to slavery'. 1492 is the conquerors' date, not that of the native populations. It is not the memory of a blessing, but the nightmare of a genocide. In Abia Yala (an indigenous name for Latin America, which means 'mature land') peoples already existed 40,000 years ago. Great cultures grew up here, with bodies of sages, sophisticated understanding in astronomy, agriculture and medicine, and with elaborate languages and religions. All this was considered the work of Satan. Christianity always showed sensitivity to the poor, but was implacable and ethnocentric when confronted with cultural difference. The 'other', the indigenous person, the black person, was regarded as the enemy, the pagan, the infidel. 'Just wars' were waged against them, and a 'requisition' read over them, a demand for voluntary submission. Recognition is essential, since it embodies the minimal justice we owe these 'others'. Recognition is what prevents the primary relationship being one of domination. It is recognition which imposes checks on the mechanisms of exclusion and destruction. Today what makes the victims suffer most is the fact of not being recognized, the fact that their cultures are despised, their languages banned in the schools, their religions still persecuted by the churches and their feasts mocked.

Thirdly, the victims *question* the project of European modernity, now translated on to a world scale, and the sort of mission the churches have practised and still practise. Modernity is characterized by the desire for power. The power is for domination, domination for profit. This logic has been applied savagely in Latin America and the Caribbean. Because of it, thousand-year-old cultures have been destroyed. It has left disfigured faces no longer able to cry, sunken eyes which no longer want to dream, and a pall of sadness has covered our past and our present. The science and technology which in the metropolitan countries bring liberation are here the principal instruments of dependence and of creating inequality. They create a type of culture which standardizes everything according to the interests and values of the dominant internationalized sectors and does not incorporate the accumulated experiences of the autochthonous cultures. They are condemned to be cultures of resistance rather than creative and liberating. Isn't this cumulative development which violates all ecosystems a route leading to us to the apocalypse?

The Christianity implanted here was, initially, a dream in the minds of the first missionaries, like the twelve Franciscan apostles of Mexico. They came full of the utopia of the era of the Holy Spirit and of the new humanity envisaged by Joachim of Fiore and filled out by the utopianists of the Renaissance. But they did not engage in dialogue with the religions which are the soul of a culture. They destroyed them as though exorcising Satan. The colonizers of yesterday and today dominated bodies. The missionaries conquered souls. The victims, today made aware of the humanitarian content of the gospel, ask themselves: what credibility does Christianity have left as an instrument for regenerating the cultures it helped to humiliate? Christianity can present its proofs of credibility if it adopts a perspective of liberation and firm support for all that allows the Indians, the African Americans and the new oppressed peoples to develop their identities as peoples and cultures in an autonomous and creative way. The new evangelization will be the good news of eternal life if it helps, here and now, to guarantee the lives of the oppressed and to restore the fabric of the witness cultures which still survive. This presupposes a radical critique of the Christendom model and assistance at the birth of the model of the church of the poor, which makes the victims its social base and their cause its chief pastoral concern.

Finally, the victims want to make an *original contribution* to the whole human race and to the church of Christ. But this is only possible if we, the whites in control, break with the logic of exclusion and death which has been continuing since 1492 and deepen the relationship of acceptance and support for otherness. 'We continue to be in the thick of an unjust war,' writes Aiban Waga, the indigenous theologian (a Kuna from Panama), in this issue of *Concilium*. This means not just a cultural rescue operation, but much more, a creative and liberating act by which the indigenous and African Americans themselves can find reasons for living, for establishing relations with the surrounding society, in full awareness of what they have to gain and what they have to lose in this necessary interaction. Only then will they become creators of their own liberation. One resource for this process is an appropriation of the Bible in which they learn to read it as a means of finding the presence of God and kingdom values in their own culture. In this way, with their own cultural riches, raised to a higher power by the word of revelation, they can make a contribution to the liberation of other oppressed sisters and brothers and show the rest of us other ways of being human and expressing the depth of the mystery which inhabits this world. If we deprive ourselves of the contribution which the different cultures of this sub-continent have to offer, we impoverish humanity as a whole. We cannot allow so much suffering, and five centuries of resistance, to have been completely in vain.

Then, so we believe in faith, the conditions may have been created for the prayer of the newly converted Maya to be answered: 'The day will come when the poor Indians' tears reach God; at that moment God's justice will come down and strike the world.'

Virgil Elizondo
Leonardo Boff

Translated by Francis McDonagh

Special Column 1990/5

For reasons beyond our control it was impossible to include this article in the October issue of Concilium

Prayer of the Religions in the New World Context

Hans Küng

That the Pope prayed in Assisi with Jews, Christians, Muslims, Japanese Buddhists, the Dalai Lama and representatives of other religions is still a topic for vigorous discussion: may one pray with those of other faiths? Here are some provisional considerations.

1. One can and must defend precisely this shared prayer – which without doubt was a happy initiative on the part of the Pope – both against some Catholic traditionalists and against Protestant fundamentalists. If one is convinced that, as is stated in the Second Vatican Council's Declaration on the Non-Christian Religions, God is the common 'origin . . . and . . . ultimate goal' of all humankind, and if therefore all men and women from whatever nation, region or religion form this one human race, then why should they not pray together to this their one origin and goal, to the 'one God'? So there seems to me to be a clear theological answer to the question whether one *may* pray together: people of different religions may pray together, and indeed should do so more often.

2. What is far more difficult to answer is the question *how we can* pray together. In Assisi the problem was avoided because while the representatives of all the religions were praying together at the same time and in the same place, each group, divided according to religion, prayed for itself. So it was possible to get round the problem and not to produce a common text. But what would happen if one were to pray together with

the same text (though of course in a variety of languages)? That certainly still needs a good deal of theological discussion and practical experimentation, and only in the course of time will it become evident what in particular is meaningful and what is not.

For it is difficult to establish any kind of general principles for praying together with shared texts – the relationship between the individual religions is too different for that. Here too it is important to make distinctions, since not all the world religions are at the same distance from one another. Thus it is well known that Christians and Jews have few difficulties if they want to pray psalms or other prayers from the Hebrew Bible or the Jewish tradition together. Those Christians who have already taken part in a Jewish service know that they can join in most of the prayers, even if, for example, they understand the term 'Torah' differently, in the sense of the 'spiritual law'. Conversely, some Jews might find no insuperable difficulties in, for example, joining in saying the Our Father in a Christian service, since its essential elements go back to the Hebrew Bible.

Similarly, for Christians (and Jews) there may be no theological difficulties in saying some of the fine prayers from the Qur'an with Muslims. After all, the Qur'an states that the same God spoke to Abraham, the prophets, Jesus and Muhammad. And those Christians who have joined in the impressive common prayer of Muslims know that it can make good sense for them to prostrate themselves to the one God of Abraham, even if they do not acknowledge the prophet Muhammad in the same way. Conversely, given time, there may be an increasing readiness, particularly in Diaspora Islam, in some circumstances also to pray Jewish or Christian prayers to the one all-merciful God. All this means that within the prophetic religions it might be possible also to address one and the same God through a common prayer.

3. However, outside the prophetic religions the question is even more complicated. Prayers like those of Indios to the 'Great Spirit' could certainly also be incorporated into Christian worship, as could Chinese prayers to the 'One Ruler of the World' or the 'Great Lord'. Here there is no departure from the sphere of the monotheistic understanding of God. But there are more difficulties with the prayers of Hindus, even if one limits oneself to the great monotheistic traditions of India, since in many instances it is impossible to mistake the polytheistic context. With Buddhists – and indeed also with many Hindus – one can at least share wordless meditation, which is practised by monks and laity throughout the world. However, we should be under no illusions that for all the sharing in silence, while for the moment the differences in faith are relativized, in the long run they do not level out. There are also prayers in the Buddhist tradition (Amida Buddhism), but they have quite a different status from that in the monotheistic or

polytheistic religions, which is why restraint by members of monotheistic religions is advisable here.

4. That already brings us to the decisive limit. One cannot expect the members of another religion to join in a prayer in which the specific nature of a religion, something which is quite peculiar and distinctive in a faith, is expressed. At best they would do that ritualistically or without seriousness, either to please a friend of another faith or because they were using parts of such prayers virtually without thinking.

Clearly, one cannot seriously expect Jews to end their prayers to the God of Israel with the addition *per Dominum nostrum Iesum Christum*, nor can one seriously expect a Muslim to use the trinitarian formula 'Glory be to the Father and to the Son and to the Holy Spirit'. The same goes for the other religions. Conversely, one cannot expect any Christians to join with Jews in confessing in faith that God promised them the physical land of Israel or to add to their confession of the one God a confession of the prophet Muhammad. Nor can one expect them to join Buddhist friends in a Japanese Amida temple in uttering the threefold formula of taking refuge (in the Buddha, Dharma and Sangha). Here above all prayer would not unite but divide; it would not reconcile but endanger the identity of the other.

Only God knows what may be possible in the distant future. The religions have now begun to get to know one another more closely, to exchange some spiritual experiences and to make some tentative attempts at praying together. And how long did it take, for example, for separated Christians to understand that they could at least pray together . . . ? But what is to be done in the meanwhile? Theologians and experts in religious studies may work towards bringing out the real religious convergences which exist despite all the real divergences. At the same time they may help in collecting good and usable texts from the different religions and translating them as possible prayers that might be shared. Finally, women and men all over the world must go on collecting practical experience in this sphere in order to provide mutual correction, supplementation and enrichment. For one thing is certain: the religions are not the 'origin and final goal' of all humankind; that continues to be God.

Translated by John Bowden

Towards the Fifth Centenary

Gustavo Gutiérrez

1992 is more than just a date. It is an occasion to render an account of the last five hundred years which – whether we like it or not – have determined our lives in Latin America to this day and have also been decisive for Europe and other continents. The initial event is called discovery, meeting, conquest by some; cover-up, un-meeting and invasion by others. In this process the Christian faith has been present – and absent – in various ways. The latter will be particularly taken into account in the Fourth Conference of Latin American Bishops (Santo Domingo, October 1992), which will aim to seek – as they did before at Medellín (1968) and Puebla (1979) – ways of announcing the gospel for the time to come.

This matter is engaging the attention of many people, coming from different spiritual families. Naturally their focus is different and they may take opposite positions on the historical process and a present reality whose wounds are still raw. It is a matter which primarily concerns those who live in Latin America, who are asking themselves once again in their rather short history what it means to be Latin American. The matter also concerns Europe, whose past as a colonial power still weighs on her, and it has repercussions in Africa, where population suffered an increase in the inhuman slave trade. The debate revives ancient passions and produces great anger.

History from the other point of view

We must also have the courage to read the facts from the other side of history. Here our sense of truth is at stake. In fact only historical honesty can free us from prejudices, narrowness, ignorance, fudging by interested parties, which makes our past a burdensome mortgage instead of an impulse to creativity.

Recovering our memory will make us throw out the so-called 'black legend' and 'rosy legend' as inadequate and therefore useless. Hiding what really happened during those years for fear of the truth, in order to defend entrenched privileges or – at the other extreme – by the frivolous use of mere slogans, condemns us to historical sterility. Nor does it accord with the demands of the gospel. This is how the gospel was understood by many of those who first came to proclaim it to this continent, and therefore they firmly denounced everything that went against the life-affirming will of the God of the kingdom of love and justice. This made the Peruvian Indian Guamán Poma exclaim, reproachfully but also with hope: 'And so, my God, where are you? You do not hear me to relieve your poor.'[1]

Trying to cover up the witnesses of the time to the immense destruction of persons, peoples and cultures, together with their vital links with the natural world, is like trying to cover the sun with one hand. Innumerable texts of missionaries (Dominicans, Franciscans, Augustinians, Jesuits, Brothers of Mercy and plenty more), members of the indigenous populations, bishops, chroniclers, historians of the era, have left accounts of an atrocious reality – whatever the exact figures – of a demographic collapse.[2] The memory of these events annoys the European nations very much: Spain and Portugal were present from the beginning and, in the majority, France, England and Holland a bit later; Germany only partially, Italy and other countries through some of their citizens. These countries are proud of the enterprise which they think of as civilizing and bringing the gospel.

It is historically false to claim that the evidence is only in documents inspired by Las Casas. Much of it appears earlier than the work of the great defender of the Indians, or comes from persons and areas not under to his influence, even some of his enemies, such as the Franciscan Motolinia (a missionary in Mexico). This is an attempt to confine the evidence to the ideas and presumed prejudices of 'a single man', as the famous document of Yucay (Cusco, 1571) claims,[3] when actually the facts are attested by numerous witnesses. What these accounts have in common is the *situation* they witnessed, not a reading of the same *texts*. This same ploy is used today with the same object: to cover up an unjust and challenging reality.

Perhaps Las Casas went most deeply into what happened at that time and articulated the most thorough theological reflection on these events. But in so doing he was only a *primus inter pares*, because there were many who went along with him and shared his hopes. What he did, together with an important group of friars and bishops – and a little later our Guamán Poma – was to denounce the oppression and death suffered by the inhabitants of the Indias, stating clearly it was caused by greed for gold, which scripture calls idolatry, as Fray Bartolomé himself points out. These men also declared that the injustices and ill-treatment existing before the arrival of the Europeans (facts whose cruelty we must also look squarely in the face) could not in any way legitimize the exploitation and dispossession of the Indians. These are elemental truths rooted in human rights and the Christian message. In stating this these men risked their lives, and Bishop Valdivieso in Nicaragua, for example, actually forfeited his.

These representatives of the best of Spain also risked their reputation because they were considered – and still are by those who are ignorant of the new historical writing on the period – to be holders of extreme positions and enemies of their country. Their sin was unmasking those whose behaviour brought shame on their country and made a mockery of the Christian faith they claimed to uphold. Thus in Spain and in the Indias they managed to provoke a discussion on the legitimacy of the European colonial presence and its methods which no other Old World country had the courage to undertake, in spite of their Christian and humanist pretensions. They also left us testimonies of realities that they themselves were trying to change, many of which we would not know about without their work. This was a difficult task in the circumstances of the time. We should appreciate it – with its limits and possibilities – in its historical context, as well as in its later repercussions.

Las Casas left us an important route by which to explore our past today. He told the European theologians (in particular John Major, a Scottish professor in Paris at the beginning of the sixteenth century) who had not set foot in these countries but were justifying the deeds being done in them: 'If we were Indian we should see things differently.' This is a firm recognition of otherness and a 'no' to integration by means of subjection and absorption of the inhabitants of the Indias. It is also a summons, still difficult for many people today, to change our point of view in order to understand these events.

History written from the conqueror's viewpoint has long hidden important aspects of the reality from us. The 'other' in Latin America remains 'open-veined' – to use the famous expression of the Uruguayan writer Eduardo Galeano – precisely because the poorest of its inhabitants are not recognized in the fullness of their human dignity. Their 'distance' from the present socio-economic order and the dominant culture makes the poor, the other, our neighbour before anyone else, as we have been taught from the outset of liberation theology by the parable of the Good Samaritan.[4]

This history is largely of the Indians' resistance to the foreign invasion and the contempt for human values that came with it. It was an opposition which in spite of everything managed to preserve cultural traditions and keep alive our languages, which nourish the present and are a vital element in our identity.

One way of recognizing the others' historical roots is to hold penitential celebrations among the quincentenary events (the opening of the Fourth Conference of Latin American Bishops could be an excellent occasion). It is not a question of masochistic posturing, which is ultimately barren and narcissistic. The point is that no one escapes responsibility for what the poor went through and are going through now. The Christian way of assuming this responsibility is humbly to ask forgiveness from God and the victims of history for our complicity – explicit or tacit – in the past and the present, as individuals and as church – in this situation. Seeking forgiveness means wanting life; it expresses a will to change our behaviour and reaffirms our duty to be an effective sign in the history of the kingdom of love and justice.

Not forgetting the present

However, it is important to point out that the purpose of looking back at this history is to deal with our present situation and to show solidarity with the poor today. The quincentenary must not become an invitation to put back the historical clock. Our approach to the past must be motivated not by nostalgia but by hope; not by a fixation upon former painful and traumatic occurrences, but because of present suffering and the conviction that only a people which has a memory can transform the situation it is in and build a different world. History, as Bartolomé de las Casas insisted, 'is the teacher of all things', as long as we turn to it in order to understand our own time better. We cannot remain fixed in the past. Thus J. C. Mariátegui called upon us not to get stuck in the past: "The Conquest, evil and all, was a historical fact. The Republic, such as it exists, is another historical fact. Against historical facts neither the mind's abstract speculations nor the spirit's highest ideals can do much. The history of Peru is just a piece of human history. Over four centuries a new reality has come about. The input from the West has created it. It is a fragile reality. But at any rate it is a reality. It would be excessively romantic to decide to ignore it today.'[5] We cannot remake history. It is a matter of realism.

Doubtless this approach has its risks; it must be made with respect for the temporal and cultural co-ordinates of the past. Impatience to learn from history sometimes leads us to manipulate it, pretending, for example, that conditions and opinions repeat themselves just as they are. These are facile comparisons which do not take the density of history into account and prevent us from looking at present challenges with fresh eyes. So unless we broaden the term excessively, we cannot call certain sixteenth-century missionaries and theologians 'liberation theologians' (an expression which has a precise contemporary meaning), as if we were giving them a medal. Saying that someone in the past was brilliant intellectually because he thought in his time as we do today is to allow ourselves to be contaminated by the arrogance of the modern spirit. Modernity considers itself supreme in history, hence its greatest praise for contributions by thinkers in previous eras of humanity is to say 'they were ahead of their time'. That is, they were 'modern' before their time . . .

For example, calling Las Casas a liberation theologian can of course draw attention to certain aspects of his thinking, but it unwittingly obscures others. So we think such a title neither appropriate nor necessary to appreciate his thought and testimony. This took place in a context very different from our own; both at the social and the theological level the language is also different. Its depth comes from its gospel roots and from the way in which Las Casas keeps faith with his Lord. Approaching this witness to God's love in our continent means respecting him in his world, his time, his sources, and being clear about his limitations. This attitude does not distance us from his work but brings us closer, without trying to abuse it to serve our present way of defending causes, which indeed have the same root. Therefore we must be able to confront new challenges in our own way, while at the same time we must learn from men like Pedro de Cordoba, Juan de Zumarraga, Vasco de Quiroga, Juan del Valle, Guamán Poma and so many others who lived and worked in these lands.

Our interest and our protest at what happened in the sixteenth century to the different Indian nations and cultures should not make us overlook the events of the centuries that came afterwards with the arrival of new races and cultures, or the exploitation and dispossession of the poor in our subcontinent today. It would be very wrong if the quincentenary confined us to the sixteenth century.

Today among the poor, as José Maria Arguedas puts it, 'all bloods' are represented. This creates a very different state of affairs from that confronting the Indians – and those in solidarity with them – in the past. But their testimony has much to teach us about how to respond to the challenges and social conflicts of our own time. Today too there is destruction of people and cultures and we go on hearing 'the just cries which have universally risen to heaven', as Tupac Amaru II said in eighteenth century Peru, when he rebelled against the colonial order.

In Latin America, to contrast, as some have begun to do, the Indian with the poor is a subtle form of remaining anchored in the past, even though claiming to adopt a new position. We can only be glad that these people are now discovering those who are marginalized in our society, because for so long they were unconcerned about them except as objects of study. Criticism of what is unilateral and squalid in certain current social analyses which ignore the racial question is valid and should be retained. But we should not separate aspects that mutually imply one another, and precisely because they do not fuse, concur to show us the complexity of the world of the poor, dispossessed and despised. This is an enrichment which we must keep. Making our task easier by picking and choosing when it is not possible to do so takes us away from the real people, their social and cultural universe as well as from their sufferings, claims and hopes today.

It is urgent that we should build a society in accordance with the interests and values of the poor today, social classes and races and cultures that are dispossessed and marginalized, women, and especially those who belong to these sectors of society. The great cultural and ethnic variety of Latin America must be welcomed without trying to impose a single cultural form, the Western, which arrived very late, as *the* culture of the region. To claim that Western culture brings the gospel is to ignore the church's experience of Pentecost. According to the Acts of the Apostles the miracle of Pentecost did not consist in speaking a single language; rather, those who had come from different racial and cultural areas heard the apostles speaking 'each in *his own language*'. This was not uniformity, but dialogue and unity based on respect for difference. It was not imposed integration, but acceptance of otherness, and ethnic and cultural heterogeneity. The process designated by the neologism 'inculturation' is highly necessary. For a Christian it also has resonances of incarnation, and therefore of authentic and profound presence in history. So concern for our present situation cannot be absent in our approach to our past. In the history of today, Christians decide on their discipleship and solidarity with the poor and oppressed.

With boldness

Reading history from the other side and in the light of our current concerns means seeking truth and solidarity. We must also add a perspective of future and of hope.

The present acquires density when it is nourished by the memory of a journey, when it has the courage to identify the problems that have not been solved and which therefore need great efforts now. This is what is happening in Latin America with the racial question. As we know, one of our great social lies is saying that there is no racism in this sub-continent. Of course we do not have racist laws. But given the small weight of the law among us, this has little significance. However, we have something much worse and much more difficult to eradicate: entrenched racist customs. Anything coming from an Indian, black or Amazonian background is an object of frivolous interest and, with important exceptions, is despised and marginalized. 'They made you an anonymous collective without face or history,' as the poet-bishop Pedro Casaldaliga expressively puts it, speaking of those who have felt this disdain and 'blanking' for centuries. Racism is undoubtedly an important component in the diverse and cruel situation of violence (institutional, terrorist, repressive) experienced today in Latin America.

We have to take the present as we find it and deal with the situation as it is and not as we might wish it to be. We have to deal with the unfinished process of non-meetings and forced meetings between races and cultures, in the present poverty and injustice suffered by the majorities. We must also be clear who are the agents in the liberating force at work among us. It is too complex to oversimplify into separate Hispanic and indigenous trends.

This is a society in the process of becoming. Its ancient wounds still have not healed, and it has trampled peoples and cultures underfoot. And even today most of its members suffer poverty and dispossession as they struggle to affirm their dignity as persons. In this society the church is called to a 'new way of preaching the gospel', to which it has been committed since Medellín.[6] This call has been taken up with vigour and clarity by John Paul II in the perspective of the quincentenary.[7] But this new preaching still requires the testimony of the great gospel preachers of the past. They were great defenders of the Indians, nor could they fail to be. We have already noted that this produces disagreement among us, and it also did in their time. That is inevitable. To speak from the standpoint of the poor, with them and not just for them, always means threatening privileged interests, as long as the enormous unjust inequalities and oppression exist.

The new gospel-preaching will have to address the challenges with which past and present history of the sub-continent present it. The discussion that arose around Medellín became sharper round Puebla, and it gains new urgency as we approach the fourth conference of Latin American bishops. Once again the debate will be fruitful, always supposing of course, that it takes on the new conditions, challenges and reflections. Latin America is too large and diverse to be explained by summary analyses.

We have to overcome the temptation – through exhaustion, fear or interest – to overlook the real challenges from a cruel, complex and painful reality. The church must listen to all the voices trying to make themselves heard in Latin America. It is an excellent opportunity to survey the whole of that history bursting upon us today. Not everything in the present is synthesis and soil waiting for the seed of the gospel, only threatened by recent and alien ideas connected with modern society, as some people seem to think. Contemporary factors as well as a disputed history play their part.

Culture is permanent creativity, It cannot be defended as tradition if it is not at the same time thrusting forward. The daily life of the poor is, in spite of everything, a permanent source of hope. It ensures that joy does not vanish. For the prophet Joel (1.12), the absence of joy was the major sign of the deep crisis afflicting his nation.

The presence of the church in this process has its 'lights and shades', as Medellín said. But over these last two decades, the experiences, reflections and testimonies of many Christians constitute a great richness with which to face our task. The new gospel-preaching to the sub-continent began during these years. They have seen the development of a church able to confront the reality in which it has to announce the gospel message, and a new way of being Christian. Both these must continue to grow. The resistance and ignorance to be found today in some church circles is a cause for concern because they are opposing the most fruitful recent tendencies in pastoral work and theology in Latin America.

We do not want merely to repeat what has been discovered or done during this time. We should avoid confusing radicalness with intellectual laziness and lack of determination to innovate and learn. A great creative force is necessary to confront the present challenges. What has been done in Latin America, for example in theology, during these decades must be rethought and reformulated, incorporating other themes and perspectives. Faithfulness to the God of our faith and to the poor implies a permanent tension between the gospel and walking with a people who are living in a changing situation.

In all this there are obvious successes, but there are still many more numbers of things that remain to be done and to change, including those within the church. Therefore Puebla calls all Christians and the church as a whole to conversion. This cannot be achieved without an attitude that the Acts of the Apostles at the dawn of missionary work in the Christian community calls *parrhesia*. This Greek term means boldness, outspokenness, the opposite of the timidity we see at present in so many church circles. There is no other way to preach the gospel. The times call us to confront the present challenges with *parrhesia*. This is based on hope in the Lord who is the truth, who – according to Las Casas – 'has a very vivid memory of the most forgotten and the littlest' and 'makes everything new' (Rev. 21.1). This newness will also affect our Latin American identity and our way of proclaiming – amid a reality marked by untimely and unjust death – the kingdom of life.

Translated by Dinah Livingstone

Notes

1. *El Primer Nueva Crónica y Buen Gobrieno* (a work written at the beginning of the seventeenth century). I quote from the Siglo XXI Press edition, Mexico 1980, p. 1104.

2. In the Pontifical Commission for Justice and Peace document, *The Church and Racism* (1988), we read: 'The first great wave of European colonization was in fact accompanied by massive destruction of the pre-Columbian civilizations and by the brutal subjection of their inhabitants. Although the great sailors of the fifteenth and sixteenth centuries may have been free from racial prejudices, the soldiers and traders did not practise the same respect. They killed in order to establish themselves; they reduced the "Indians" to slavery to use them as man power, as they did later the blacks, and developed a racist theory in order to justify themselves' (n. 3).

3. Cf. on this text G. Gutiérrez, *Dios o el Oro en las Indias Siglo XVI*, Lima 1989.

4. Cf. G. Gutiérrez, *A Theology of Liberation*, Maryknoll and London ²1989, pp. 113–15.

5. *Peruanicemos al Peru*, Lima 1970, p. 66.

6. Cf. the message of the conference (and also the preparatory document).

7. Speech in Haiti (October 1983). In fact the Pope had already used the expression 'new gospel-preaching' in Poland (speech in the city of Nova Huta, 9 June 1981). Cf. Cecilia Tovar, 'Juan Pablo II y la nueva evangelización', in *Páginas* 102, Lima, April 1990, pp. 35–54.

I · The Traumatic Memory of the Conquest

The Latin American People

Darcy Ribeiro

The commemoration of the quincentenary sometimes takes on a detestable tone of celebration and glorification of the achievements of the conquest. More acceptable, because well intentioned, is the plausible talk of those who, instead of conquest, invasion or clash, speak about a meeting of civilizations to describe what was the most terrible failure to meet in the history of humanity; a battle royal, as an Indian intellectual said. I do not like the demagogy of those who claim that in the invasion of the Americas there were neither winners nor losers. It is clear that there were and still are. The Indians have been humiliated and oppressed for five centuries. A minimum of respect for their tragedy should be enough to silence these irresponsible voices.

If there is anything to celebrate in this quincentenary, it is, on the one hand, the centuries of resistance of the Indians, who, fighting against all the odds, remain, where they survive, Indians, maintaining their ethnic identity. On the other hand, there is the product of this terrible process of genocide and ethnocide: we, the 500 million Latin Americans.

The shock of Columbus' encounter or clash with the New World – and this is the only thing that makes it a discovery – was the sudden realization that it existed. It was there, it had existed in its own right from time immemorial, this whole world of which the Western world was unaware.

Its existence was suspected, it is true, but people imagined some sort of magic concealment, anti-islands, or the miraculous lands of fire shown on old maps. But in its self-sufficiency the ill-named Old World had grown blind to the inconceivable, the independent existence of any relevant entity of which it was unaware. When the news spread, its first effect was total confusion, immediately replaced by the arrogance of thinking that Europeans had not only discovered, but, in discovering, invented or even created, a New World.

In fact, for Europeans, even though it existed, it was as though it did not exist until, finally fulfilling an inevitable destiny, it emerged from concealment. And this took place thanks to the eyes of Columbus, who had been sent for that express purpose. He, still not knowing what he was seeing, with no attempt to assess its size, supposed that these few islands he had found were the true Eastern Indies, if they were not the Lost Paradise itself, such was the beauty of the land and the innocence of the naked Indian women.

The conquest

From that moment another question presented itself, an essentially practical question: what value could there be in this whole world of endless lands and countless exotic peoples which was gradually revealed? Not value in themselves, because this did not count. The value would be the mere exercise of their existence as they were, which in the eyes of the invaders was no justification, and even a scandal in its uselessness. No, what value for Europe, which thought of itself as owner of a universe in which the whole and each of its parts could only exist to serve it, expanding its dominions, submitting to its faith and, above all, working for its prosperity?

So there then began the demolition of that vast mass of peoples, civilizations and cultures, as independent and distinct forms of human existence, who then had to reconstruct themselves on the ruins as the opposite of themselves, under the control of a foreign, hostile master.

In a second stage, when the Europeans had worn out the peoples they found here, they fetched millions of other strange peoples from among the black peoples of Africa to feed their people-mill and produce exportable wealth. Later, when the European proletariat, outgrowing the labour needs of Europe's productive system, became in its turn an export commodity, a wave of gringo whiteness came also to settle in the Americas.

It was in this process that the world became unified, attaining existence and destiny through the action of Europe, which brought together under its command the Eastern Old World – an object of pillage – and the neighbouring and familiar African World – so far useless, tying both of them to what was or was to be the New World of America.

In this way the earth and its innumerable peoples, a great part of the human race, were converted into a colonial possession and a profitable business, and acquired a new destiny. They were no longer to exist and be themselves, so doubling the potential of human activity, but to refashion themselves according to European dictates, defined by the profit motive. Step by step, Europe imposed its hegemony and, where it could, its own being, on the two ancient provinces and the new one – each of which had its own original civilization and had existed in its own right from time immemorial. In so doing it interrupted the flow of their histories and made them crumble from existence into non-existence, or into existence for others: that is, an existence governed by commercial calculations performed in the capitals of Europe for Europe's benefit.

The powerful motor of this huge business – profit –, which directed the process of expansion, was never explicitly mentioned. It disguised its motives so well that it succeeded in convincing even the leaders of the conquest that they were obeying lofty spiritual inspirations and fulfilling sacred destinies in the plan of salvation by carrying out new crusades for Christendom. It is true that there were always people who took care from the very beginning to clothe the acquisition of new worlds in the necessary legality. So, a year after Columbus' arrival, the Holy Father was already extending to the Americas the privileges to rule over lands and enslave peoples which had been granted for Africa and Africans as early as the beginning of 1454.

Spaniards and Portuguese performed their feats in the name of Christendom, trying to believe that they were fulfilling a sacred destiny of freeing the Indians from idolatry and heresy in order to save at least their souls for eternal life. Their bodies they wore out with exemplary efficiency. By as early as the end of the first century after the conquest the original American population had been reduced from around ninety million to less than ten, by war and white plagues, but above all by slavery.

Possessed by the same holy fury, they demolished temples more majestic than any in Europe at the time, and burnt as works of the devil the thousands of books of Mayan wisdom, of which all that survive are a few manuscripts priceless for the beauty, devotion and wisdom they reveal. The same fate befell the countless *quipos* which contained the Inca records. Their works of art, accused of being sinful idolatry, were destroyed or melted down into rich ingots, if made of gold, silver or platinum.

The protagonists

The persecution continued in the subsequent centuries, on a different scale, it is true, but with the same aim of bringing civilization by imposing Christianity and European values. There was no longer the splendour of the former pillage of priceless wealth because the Indians had been stripped of all their wealth, and their survivors became pariahs. They have become merely a labour force exploited to the utmost, barely managing to survive on the lands in which they once built civilizations, or tribes who have brought flight to a fine art, constantly moving beyond the frontier of civilization in order to escape from it.

The astounding miracle of their indigenous resistance is showing us that ethnic identity is one of the most powerful forces in history. It is capable both of resistance by fighting for centuries and of disguising itself so as to remain invisible and unnoticed; but all the time the group retains within itself its own being, its own face and its pride in being those unique and irreducible people that they are. An ethnic group is indeed indelible, and will survive as long as parents are able to bring up their children in the tradition in which they were brought up.

Confronted with this sometimes amazing resistance, the first question which arises is to establish for certain who it was who wreaked this murderous fury. We have to assess how far we Latin Americans of today and yesterday are the real oppressors, following our Iberian ancestors, who continue to persecute and massacre the Indians. The truth is that the main actors in the post-conquest period were no longer Spanish and Portuguese, but us. We neo-Americans were and are the butchers of the Indians, both of those who were exterminated and of those who survive but are still treated as foreigners and freaks in their own land.

Until recently the great mass of Indians surviving from the great American civilizations were regarded as a peasantry who would one day, with a decent agrarian reform, give up their fantasy of being Indians and integrate into Creole society. The small tribal groups, too, were seen as obsolete survivals doomed to disappear. Today we realize that these indigenous groups are oppressed peoples fighting for the right to control their own future, and that these miraculously surviving tribal groups are not dying out but, on the contrary, are beginning to increase their populations. Both groups are involved in struggle, both against their direct oppressors and exploiters and also against their supposed official and priestly protectors who, full of generous words, in truth seek to destroy them.

But destroying them is impossible, because these people, who have survived centuries of intentional ethnocide and genocide, will not succumb now, when the Europeanizers' weapons are weaker. It is even more impossible because, following the worldwide trend which is reaching the oppressed peoples of the whole earth, the American Indians, too, are rising to drive out their supposed protectors, reject the oppressive legislation which governments impose on them, and take on their own defence.

One of the most powerful weapons in the persecution of the Indians is the old civilizing hypocrisy of allegedly protective measures, such as the laws protecting Indians, especially those which guarantee them possession of the lands on which they live. Brazilian law is a perfect example of this. It is written into the constitution and leaves no room for improvement, but Indians continue to be deprived of their land. Twenty Indian leaders have been murdered in recent years, but rarely has a killer been brought to trial, and none has been imprisoned. Religious missions continue to invade villages, preaching evangelical harangues in their centuries-old endeavour to make the indigenous peoples Christian by making them European. Such fervour would make sense if it was not well known that after centuries of this crazed and constant zeal for conversion, no Indian has ever been converted.

The Jesuits recognized, after less than ten years of evangelization, that no one converts anyone. One of the first missionaries, Manoel da Nóbrega, used to say, 'I'll convert them with a fish-hook, but with two I'll unconvert them.' After a massive investment in catechesis they concluded that conversion, the light of faith, is only kindled in human hearts by the will of God. The missionaries' harvest, they used to think, was the grace of their own sanctity, if possible through a yearned-for martyrdom, which they cultivated alongside the Indians, very often in the most oppressive form of ethnocide.

Catholics since John XXIII have become more aware of this insanity, and the church itself is trying to check the evangelizing obsessions of its more fanatical missionaries. Not the Protestants: they persist in the same mindless and perverse fantasy of promoting European culture through Christianity, with no respect for indigenous identity, which is for them no more than the space in which they exercise their missionary fervour, fulfilling what they believe to be the will of God.

In my forty years of contact with indigenous peoples I have never seen any tribe converted, and many of them have suffered decades of missionary activity: the Borôro, for example; or even centuries, like the Guarani. When conversion occurs, it never takes place as a result of the efforts of missionaries, but through a desperate search for a new spirituality by people disorientated by the vicissitudes of life. This is what happens to the children of Indian women brought up by non-Indians: having lost their own being and identity, they attempt to construct another self-image as human beings, and in that quest from time to time surrender themselves to millenarian cults: the Tikuna, for example; or to salvationist devotions: the Xokleng, for example. Or they become genuinely incorporated into some faction of Christendom in the diaspora, as in the case of the Terena and the Xavante, Catholics and Protestants respectively.

The almanac

The 1992 commemorations may perhaps help to deepen awareness of this long-drawn-out clash which is still continuing. In countries like Guatemala, where it survives, the Maya civilization is fighting to create its own structures, against the mass of native *mestizos* as cruel in their anti-indigenous rage as the sixteenth-century Spaniards. Or on the border between Brazil and Venezuela the last Amazonian forest people, the Yanomami, see their villages invaded by thousands of gold-miners and record the arrival of civilization in their bodies rotted by unknown diseases.

The only force capable of helping either the modern Maya or the primeval Yanomami is world public opinion. Accordingly, mobilizing world opinion is the greatest task facing those who want to celebrate or commemorate the sixteenth-century invasion and the events it set in motion.

The other side of the question is one which can be summed up in the proposition: the 500 years, from 1492 to 1992, mean 500 million Latin Americans, the most substantial new presence in the body of humanity. The main result of the civilizing process which took place in these five centuries was our emergence. This is the real, palpable result of the movement initiated with the European expansion, which, in order to bring us into being, extinguished, snuffed out, thousands of peoples with their original languages and cultures, and exterminated at least three great civilizations.

We are the children of the prodigious reproduction of a few Europeans and a handful of Africans, carried out in millions of wombs of indigenous women, kidnapped and many times raped. Disloyal children who, though rejected by their parents as impure because of mixed race, never identified with their maternal stock; on the contrary, they became their most effective and hateful oppressors and chastizers. So true is this that, as well as the tragedy of the conquest, we must turn our anger against the equal tragedy of the later domination, which extended for centuries and centuries and is still being savagely maintained. This is the basis of Latin American society and its growth; it draws its life, its support and its prosperity from the constant wearing down of the indigenous peoples.

It is out of these culturally impoverished, parentless *mestizos* that we were formed in a continuing ethnocide directed by the most hideous Eurocentrism. Shaped by foreign hands and wills and reshaped by ourselves, with the spurious and alienated consciousness of a colonial population, we were made not to be, not to appear and never to recognize who we really are.

This is the source of our constant search for identity as an ambiguous people, no longer indigenous, nor African nor European, but still not accepting ourselves proudly as the New People we are. We may not be a better people than others, but we are at least more human, being formed from the most varied types of humanity. We are a people which over the centuries has suffered the most brutal and constant poverty and oppression, still heavily soiled by fantasies of Europe, still bearing in abundance the scars of slavery and colonialism, still very badly served by alienated and faithless intellectuals; but we are a people already opening up to the future, already on the march to create its own civilization, driven by an insatiable hunger for fullness, happiness and joy.

Even greater than the holocaust of the conquest was, as we have seen, that which followed in the subsequent centuries and produced two new categories of humankind. Both are impressive, in number and also in the staggering homogeneity of their cultures.

One of these, the Neo-Britannic, contributed nothing new to the world, but was simply the transplantation and expansion of the life-styles and countrysides of their countries of origin to the vast spaces of the New World. The Neo-Latin, in contrast, was wholly new because it was created by racial and cultural mixing with the original American peoples, with the addition of a huge black component.

So we came to be, New Peoples, born of the de-Indianization, de-Europeanization and de-Africanization of our origins. But this took place as part of a process dominated by assimilationism instead of apartheid. Here racial mixing has never been seen as a sin or a crime. Quite the reverse, our prejudice has always lain precisely in the general expectation that blacks, Indians and whites would not keep themselves apart, but blend one with another to produce a brown society, a mixed-race civilization.

That is why, confronted by the clamour of those who are celebrating the quincentenary of that inaugural event, my position is diametrically opposed to that of those who only draw attention to the genocide and ethnocide of the conquest. They see heroic achievement or horror and either propose nostalgic commemorations of the past greatness of the invaders or call meetings to give a voice to the survivors of the original indigenous populations.

It is not bad that this should be done. It is understandable that Spain, still harried by tales of its crimes, should want to display the greatest achievement in its history. It is also understandable that Italy should want to display its clean hands in homage to Columbus and Vespucci, insisting that they never produced a Prospero.

But we Latin Americans cannot join this dance of glories and macabre reminiscences. Those horrors were the birth-pangs which brought us into the world. What deserves attention is not only the blood shed, but also the creature conceived and born in it. Without us, Romanness would be reduced to the numerical insignificance of the Neo-Latin races of Europe, of no weight in a world overfull of Neo-British, Slavs, Chinese, Arabs, etc., etc.

The glory of Iberia, and it is well that we should stress it here, lies in its having preserved for over a millennium the seeds of Roman civilization under Gothic and Saracan oppression, and multiplied it here on a vast scale. We are the Latin American people, the largest component of Latin civilization, preparing to realize their potential. It will be a Latin culture renewed and improved, because clothed in Indian and black flesh and heir to the practical wisdom of the peoples of the forest and the high plains, of the Andean plateaux and the southern seas.

Configurations

In my classification of modern extra-European peoples I distinguish four different categories, in terms of their historical and cultural formation.

The first of these is the *Transplanted Peoples*, formed by the expansion of the European nations across overseas territories but without mixing with the local population; they reconstructed their old countryside and returned to their previous patterns of life. Subsequently they developed culturally along lines parallel and similar to those of their motherlands, as overseas white peoples. Examples are New Zealand and Australia. Argentina and Uruguay also fall into this category, although to a lesser degree, since both nations became Europeanized only after they had formed as peoples of mixed race and as such built their states and gained independence. The process took place in a subsequent cultural transformation brought about by the weight of European immigration they experienced.

In this configuration the Transplanted Peoples regard themselves proudly as the representatives and heirs of Western European civilization; they are both beneficiaries and victims of their own expansion. They are the most modern peoples and, as such, those who have come nearest to losing their features and distinctiveness. In consequence they are today of all human beings the most literate, the most standardized and most uniform, and also the most uninteresting and insipid.

In second place are the *Witness Peoples*, consisting of the present-day survivors of original high civilizations with which European expansion collided but which it was unable to graft on to its stock and assimilate. This category includes the Indians, the Muslims, the Chinese, the Indo-Chinese, the Japanese, etc. In the Americas they are represented by Mexico, Peru and Bolivia and Guatemala.

Each of these Witness Peoples has experienced enormous vicissitudes and undergone heavy Europeanization, but not enough to weld them into an entity which could make the whole population an ethnic unity. They live the tension of the ambiguity of peoples situated between two opposed cultural worlds, without being able to embrace either. They are no longer indigenous, but they will never be Europeans. The resultant civilization will confront them with an immense challenge on the cultural plane, that of shedding a false image of unity to enable each of their ethnic components to accept its own identity and take on the independent direction of its destiny and enjoy a renaissance.

The third category, *New Peoples*, are those populations deriving from racial mixing and cultural interchange between whites and blacks or tribal Indians, with the whites in control. Such peoples include the Brazilians, the Colombians, the Venezuelans and the Cubans. Their distinctive feature is that they are de-cultured peoples who have lost their specific Indian, African or European characteristics and become a new ethnic group.

Compared with the Transplanted Peoples, mere overseas Europeans, as opposed to the Witness Peoples, who carry two cultural heritages which will never mix, the New Peoples are a sort of unprogrammed stock, having been deprived of their paltry original endowment. Detached from pasts without glory or greatness, they have only a future. Their achievement is not in the past, but to come. Their only boast is, despite all vicissitudes, to have formed themselves into vast peoples homogeneous in language, culture and race. Summing up in themselves the virtues and the vices of all races and castes of humanity, they are called to create a new human condition, perhaps one of greater solidarity.

There is no doubt that in the shaping of each New People the dominant element, as a result of colonial rule, was the European, which gave them an Iberian language and a degraded version of Iberian culture. Nevertheless the culture absorbed so many elements surreptitiously infiltrated by indigenous and African cultures that they acquired a characteristic and unmistakable stamp.

For a long time the élites of the New Peoples regarded themselves as Europeans in exile. Their intellectuals would only be consoled for living in the tropics by catching the glitter of Parisian life. Poisoned by European racism, they resented their brown faces. It is only in recent times that there has arisen a general awareness that they are something else, as different from Europe as they are from indigenous America and black Africa. Nonetheless there are still plenty of mindless nonentities in these parts who pretend to be what they are not, gushing and parroting the smart talk of Europe.

From the Indians the New Peoples received two substantial inheritances. The first was the ecological formula for survival in the tropics, based on thousands of years of adaptive effort by the indigenous peoples, who taught the whites how to produce the material conditions for the existence of their societies. The second was a huge genetic contribution. The so-called 'white' in the populations of the New Peoples is fundamentally a person of mixed race sired by European men in the wombs of indigenous women. Since the number of men was always very small, these populations are genetically much more indigenous than Caucasian.

From the blacks the New Peoples also received an important genetic contribution, which varies from place to place according to the extent of black slavery, and which has made them mulatto as well as *mestizo*. The black cultural contribution is represented essentially by those features which were able to survive under the oppression of slavery. These range from skills and values to feelings, rhythms, musical qualities, tastes and beliefs which the black slaves were able to lock away within themselves and so preserve from enslavement.

Today these qualities have made characteristics such as vigour, cheerfulness and creativity distinctive features of the New Peoples who have incorporated the largest numbers of blacks. So deep and complete was the process of acculturation of the blacks that their presence is visible less in African characteristics than by the extraordinary creativity which is giving them an increasing influential role in the cultural life of their nations.

The fourth historico-cultural category in my typology is that of *Emergent Peoples*. This applies to the ethnic groups which are now appearing in Europe, Africa and Asia, and in the Americas, and occupying the space newly available for the reconstruction of autonomous and distinctive cultural identities. It is these distinctions which give the New Peoples whatever uniqueness they possess.

Does Latin America exist?

Once, in reply to an ill-mannered Englishwoman who doubted whether Latin America existed, I argued at length to prove that, thanks be to God, we do exist. I argued forcefully. We exist as a people, indeed, capable of good, since we have no wish and no need to take anything from anyone, being formed of men and women from so many different latitudes and of every race.

In geographical terms it is a truism that Latin America is a unity in the sense of a continuous continent. However, this physical basis is not matched by any unified socio-political structure, or by an active or co-operative co-existence. The immensity of the continent breaks down into individual nationalities, some of them a very inadequate framework for a people to realize its potential.

The truth is that geographical unity never functioned as a unifying factor here, because the different colonial implantations which gave rise to Latin American societies coexisted without cooperating for several centuries. Each of them had a direct relationship with the colonial metropolis. Even today we Latin Americans live as if we were an archipelago of islands joined by sea and air, and tend to look outward, towards the great world economic centres, rather than inward. Even Latin American frontiers, which run along the wastes of the Andean chain or through impenetrable jungle, isolate more than they join and rarely encourage close contact.

In terms of language and culture we Latin Americans form a group as homogeneous or as diverse as the Neo-Britannic world of those peoples who mainly speak English. To those who talk about Latin America as a definite, uniform and active entity, that statement may seem to do the region less than justice, but they forget that the category of 'Latin American' includes, among others, Brazilians, Mexicans, Haitians and the implant of French Canada, each as different from each other, despite a basic linguistic uniformity, as are the North Americans from the Australians or Afrikaners. Merely to list the components shows how broad the two categories are and how little classificatory power they have.

If we narrow the focus to 'Iberians', we find a more substantial unity. Nonetheless, even this is not much more homogeneous, since it excludes only the descendants of French colonization. It retains the Argentines, Cubans, Puerto Ricans, Chileans, etc., though from the point of view of each of these nationalities, their own national identity has much more distinctiveness and substance than the common denominator which makes them all Ibero-Americans.

If we focus down still more, we can distinguish two contrasting categories: a Luso-American component concentrated exclusively in Brazil, and a Hispano-American component which covers all the rest. The differences between the two are at least as relevant as the differences between Portugal and Spain. This shows how insignificant they are, since they are based on a small linguistic variation which is not enough to be an obstacle to communication, even though we tend to exaggerate it because of our common, intertwined but often turbulent history.

Similarities and differences

Looking again at Latin America as a whole, one notes various presences and absences which give colour and diversity to the picture. For example, the indigenous presence in Guatemala and the Andean *altiplano* is famous; there this presence is a majority, and in Mexico it is numbered in millions, and predominates in certain regions. In these cases the mass of the survivors of the original indigenous population who have become incorporated into the individual national societies as an ethnically distinct peasantry is so large that it must inevitably one day emerge as autonomous peoples. This means that in the years to come countries such as Guatemala, Bolivia, Peru and Ecuador, and large areas of others such as Mexico and Colombia, will experience far-reaching social upheavals of an ethnic character which will redefine those national units or restructure them as federations of independent peoples.

There is a totally different situation in the other countries, where there are no more than tiny tribal groups submerged in vast and ethnically homogeneous national societies. In these cases, a visible indigenous presence, whether in language, as in the case of Guarani in Paraguay, or, and more importantly, in the physical appearance of the majority of the population, as is the case in Brazil, Chile and Venezuela, must be a different category of Indo-Americans from that suggested above. It is unlikely that these cases will lead to an explicative typology.

The aborigines are a formative genetic and cultural element in all these peoples, but their contribution was so thoroughly absorbed that, whatever the fate of the surviving indigenous populations, the overall ethnic make-up will not alter greatly. In other words, miscegenation, absorption and Europeanization of the old indigenous groups within the general population are either complete or in progress, and are tending to homogenize, though not to obliterate, all ethnic features, converting them into different modes of participation in the same national ethnic group.

This does not mean that the Indians who have survived as tribes in these countries will eventually disappear. On the contrary, though increasingly adopting cultural features of the surrounding society, they will survive as distinct gorups and steadily increase in numbers.

An additional distinctive element, contributing its own features to the picture, is the presence of blacks from Africa, who are heavily concentrated along the areas of the Brazilian coast first colonized and in mining areas, and in addition in the West Indies, where sugar plantations flourished. Outside these regions there are various pockets of black presence in Venezuela, Colombia, the Guyanas, Peru and some areas of Central America.

In the case of blacks, absorption and assimilation have gone even further, and this group has been Americanized much more completely than the others. This is because the surviving Africans were left no escape route or chance of return, such as was available to Indians or Europeans. All they could do was further deepen their Latin Americanness. It is true that reminiscences of Africa are strong in folklore, music and religion in the areas where the influx of Africans was greatest, but their persistence is to be explained mainly by the marginalized state of these groups, which never constituted ethnic blocs resistant to assimilation or longing for either autonomy or repatriation.

Other distinctive non-European presences, such as the Japanese in Brazil or the Chinese in Peru or the Indians in the West Indies, also make a difference to some areas, giving a special flavour to their cooking and making their mark in some other areas. The noteworthy point about these cases – as about that of the blacks – is that they are groups with inherent racial features which differentiate them from the rest of the population.

This fact has obvious consequences. The main one is that it hinders recognition of an assimilation which is already complete, or only not complete because of the persistence of racial features which make it possible for others to go on treating as Afro, *nissei*, Chinese or Indian individuals who are such only in their physical appearance, but otherwise are completely acculturated and fully integrated into the national ethnic structure. Anthropologists who are particularly interested in the distinctive features of these communities have produced a vast literature which perhaps gives excessive weight to these differences. Indeed, it is possible to produce long lists of cultural survivals which connect these groups to their origins.

Even in this case, however, the truth is that the similarities are more important than the differences, since all these groups are fully 'Americanized'. On the linguistic and cultural levels they are natives of their countries, and even count as 'ours' in the everyday emotional identification of the rest of the population. Their distinctive features, which are perhaps tending to fade, merely make them distinctive members of the national community because of their remote origin.

The same is true of the various members of the non-Iberian European contingents which have arrived in more recent periods. Each of these represents a particular form of participation, neither superior nor inferior, in the national body, and allows them to be defined, restrictively, as, for example, Anglo-Uruguayans, Italo-Argentines, Germano-Chileans or Franco-Brazilians. It should be noted, however, that they all enjoy a higher social status, the result perhaps of cultural and economic advantages, but mainly of greater social acceptance in societies dominated by whites.

For all that unifying factors outweigh factors of differentiation, certain visible differences frequently come to be identified with social discrimination. Dark skin, for example, coincides with poverty, which gives rise to a social stratification apparently based on race. The black and indigenous groups who had to face enormous obstacles to rise from the status of slaves to that of proletariat are concentrated in the poorer strata of the population.

In addition to the poverty deriving from the exploitation of which they were, and still are, victims, they have to suffer a great deal of discrimination, including that arising out of the general expectation that they will continue to occupy subordinate positions, which hinders their rise to higher positions in the social scale.

The causal factor in this discrimination appears to be racial origin and the presence of its physical stigma, when in fact its explanation is merely the vicissitudes of the historical process, which placed them in the position of victims. They are the deprived counterparts of the Euro-Americans. Though they constitute the bulk of the labour force – or precisely because of this, being descendants of slaves – they are treated with disdain and indifference. In this way skin colour and other racial features typical of blacks and indigenous people, functioning as indicators of low status, continue to be a trigger for the prejudice which affects them.

Though present in Latin America, and sometimes very strong, racial prejudice here does not take on the discriminatory and isolating character found, for example, in the United States. There discrimination affects the descendants of Africans or indigenous peoples, whatever the intensity of the racial features they display, and it tends to exclude them from social life because mixing with them is considered undesirable.

In Latin America racial prejudice is mainly about appearance and not about origin. In other words, it affects a person in proportion to distinctive racial features and implicitly encourages miscegenation, because its aim is to 'whiten' the whole population. The standard is 'brown', rather than white or black. It is clearly racial prejudice, because society admits blacks or indigenous only as future people of mixed race, rejecting their racial type as the human ideal. But it is a particular sort of prejudice in that it discriminates against indigenous or black features because they are not yet diluted within the mainly mixed-race population, whose ideal of inter-racial relationships is fusion.

Homogenity without unity

Through the criss-crossing of all the differentiating factors, the origin of the colonizers, the presence, absence and size of indigenous, African and other groups, the dominant image of the Latin American world which emerges is the unity of the product resulting from Iberian expansion across America and its successful process of homogenization. Out of all these groupings, present in greater or lesser degree in one region or another, ethnic and national societies have been built whose populations are the product of cross-breeding and wish to continue mixing. With the exception of indigenous communities deriving from the high civilizations or small tribal ethnic groups surviving in isolation, in no case do we find the original Indians; nor are the Europeans, the Asians or the Africans what they were when they left their origins.

Their descendants are neo-Americans whose vision of the world, life-styles and aspirations – in essence identical – make them one of the most variegated branches of the human species. The fusion of people from all corners of the earth has created here peoples of mixed race preserving in their ethnic and cultural features heritages drawn from all the sources of the human race.

These heritages, which spread instead of becoming concentrated in ethnic pockets, have been superimposed on the basic pattern – mainly Iberian in some countries, mainly indigenous or African in others – embellishing the Latin American mosaic without breaking it into mutually opposing elements. The main factor in this is, once again, uniformity and the process of homogenization, which includes more than 90% of Latin Americans.

This continuing homogenization is legendary in some areas, such as the linguistic and cultural. It is a fact that the languages spoken in Latin America, and the corresponding cultural systems, are much more homogeneous than those which exist in the corresponding colonial countries, and perhaps more so than in any other area of the world, except the Neo-Britannic.

The Spanish and the Portuguese spoken in the Americas have in fact suffered fewer regional variations than in their countries of origin. Spanish, spoken by hundreds of millions of people in Latin America, though covering a vast area, varies regionally only in accent; it has never diverged into a single dialect, whereas in Spain various mutually unintelligible languages continue to be spoken. The same is true of Portuguese and English. In other words, the Spaniards, Portuguese and English, who never succeeded in assimilating the linguistic and dialectic pockets of their small home territories, when they migrated to the Americas imposed on their vastly larger colonies a near-absolute linguistic uniformity and an equally striking cultural homogeneity.

And so we are back to the initial uniformity. It matters little that this is not perceived clearly in each national unit, among other reasons because each nation is an attempt to stress particularities as a means of self-glorification and self-affirmation which only mean anything to those who share the same ethnic loyalties. What is certain is that our Latin Americanness, so obvious to those who look at us from outside and see our essential macro-ethnic identity, has one flaw: it has so far not succeeded in making us an autonomous political entity, a Latin American nation or a federation of Latin American states. But it is not impossible that history should eventually do so. Bolívar's goal was to set against the Northern United States a United States of the South. Artigas' *patria grande*, the 'great homeland', and Martí's 'our America' point in the same direction.

What is the source of this unifying power? What explains the resistance to assimilation of linguistic and cultural islands like the Basque Country, Galicia or Catalonia, or the regions of Portugal which have their own dialects, in comparison with the flexibility of such varied groups as those which formed the Ibero-American peoples?

Perhaps the explanation lies in the different characteristics of the very process of the formation of our peoples, namely, its deliberate character, its prosperity and its violence. Here the colonizing powers had an explicit programme and very clear goals, and acted with total despotism. They were able, almost immediately, to subjugate the pre-existing society, paralyse the original civilizations and convert the population into a submissive labour force.

A further contribution to this homogenization came from the very prosperity of the colonial enterprise, whether in the stage of the centuries of pillage of wealth or in the various later forms of appropriation of commodity production. Such wealth allowed for the establishment of a vast military, administrative and ecclesiastical bureaucracy, which came to control every detail of social life. Productive concerns were implanted according to a careful plan. The cities grew up as the result of deliberate planning, with streets marked out according to a pre-established plan and with buildings also modelled to fit prescribed norms.

Even the ethnic and social groupings which gradually formed had their whole life regulated; there were rules about what jobs each could aspire to, what clothes and even what jewels each could wear, and whom they could marry. All these artifical and deliberate regulations were directed to a single aim: to defend and ensure the prosperity of the colony for the benefit of the colonial power. There was also a secondary aim, though presented as primary: to create an island of missionary Catholic ideology.

The dominant native classes, the managers of this colonial pact and this cultural reproduction, never formed the peak of an autonomous society. They were merely a managerial stratum which supervised and legitimized the process of colonization. Once their societies gained independence, the exogenous character of these dominant classes, stamped on them in the colonial period, led them to continue directing their nations as consuls of other empires. To this end they established an appropriate socio-economic and political system, based on large landholdings and servility to foreign capital, and promoted cultural creativity merely as a local embodiment of foreign cultural traditions.

The deliberate character of the process led on the one hand to the search for rationality, conceived as effective measures to achieve predetermined goals. On the other hand, it led to a determination to achieve goals foreign to the aspirations of the mass of the population, who were conscripted as a labour force. At no point in the process of colonization did these groups involved in production constitute a community existing in its own right, a people with its own aspirations which it could realize as elementary preconditions for its survival and prosperity. What they constituted was human fuel in the form of muscle power, to be consumed in the generation of profit.

There gradually emerged an irreducible contradiction between the programme of the colonizers and their successors and the interests of the human community resulting from colonization. In other words, there was a contradiction between the aims and methods of dominant (but also subordinate) class and the majority of the population who operated the colonial and subsequently national enterprise. For this population the challenge thrown down across the centuries has been to mature as a people in their own right, conscious of their interests and with aspirations to a share in the control of their own destiny. Because of the divergence in interests of the different classes, they had to secure these objectives by a struggle against the dominant class which managed the old social system. Because in addition to classes Latin America has a set of institutions equipped with absolute powers to perpetuate themselves, the struggle becomes eminently political. Even today it is the main challenge facing us all as Latin Americans.

To assert our identity and realize our potential, all we need to do is to free ourselves from our own mediocre and sterile dominant classes, which have made us a foreign proletariat of the First World, to be mercilessly exploited. When we emerge from the poverty and ignorance to which we have been condemned for centuries, as producers of what we do not consume in order to generate prosperity for others, we shall finally shine as the new civilization of creativity, solidarity, joy and happiness which it is our destiny to be.

Translated by Francis McDonagh

The Real Motives for the Conquest

Enrique Dussel

It will soon be four years ago that, to complete the destruction of this land, a mouth of hell was discovered, through which a vast number of people passed each year, whom the Spaniards' greed sacrifices to their God. This is a silver mine called Potosí (Letter of Domingo de Santo Tomás, later bishop of La Plata, Bolivia, 1 July 1550; *AGI* Charcas 313).

I have already written a number of articles about this period in *Concilium*;[1] in this article I shall deal simply with the topic suggested by the editors of this issue, the *'real* motives' of that event which was the conquest – if by 'real' is understood the deepest root of the actions of those 'invaders' who carried out the 'modern' expansion of Europe, which in 1992 reaches the half-millenium of this dominatory 'planetarization'. It also needs to be borne in mind that the 'conquest' followed the 'discovery', and that the two are distinct and to some extent have distinct motives – certainly the motives for the second throw light on the motives for the first.

I. The conquest is a 'European' Christian act

The first aspect I would like to stress is that, contrary to what some people think, the fact of the 'conquest' of the New World, a 'world' *absolutely* unknown to the whole of earlier Euro–Afro–Asian history, is a 'European' Christian act (and not just a Luso-Hispanic one). In terms of world history it is 'Europe' which went beyond its borders in the fifteenth century – and consequently it is Europe as a whole which benefited from the inability of Portugal and Spain to develop an industrial capitalism, as happened in other areas in the centre and north of the continent. Therefore *responsibility* for the conquest is also Christian and 'European'.

1.1 Christian Europe as 'peripheral'

It is of the utmost importance for an understanding of the global significance of the conquest of the New World to accept from the start the absolutely 'peripheral' position of Christian Europe (in terms of geography, population, history, economy, etc.) until the end of the fifteenth century.[2]

Hegel has accustomed us to explanations of world history by a movement going from east to west, following this schema (to be read from right to left):[3]

The Movement of World History (Ideological interpretation)

(A) Modern ← Europe	Middle ← Ages	Rome←Greece←Persia←India←China
(B) Modern → Period	Middle → Ages	Ancient Period

The arrows in A indicate the direction of the growth of 'freedom', 'development' and 'subjectivity', with its final axis in Christianity (in Hegel's view). The arrows in B indicate the direction of the 'unfolding': from the foundation, by a sort of 'inversion'. The movement is towards what is founded, what explains is what is realized (modern Christian Europe, England and Germany, in Hegel's view), and what comes before is its prehistory. In this way Christian 'Europe' achieves, certainly from as early as the fifteenth century (from 1492), but ideologically, philosophically and theologically from the 'Enlightenment', a 'reconstruction' of world history in which Europe projects itself backwards as the 'centre' of that history from the origin (from Adam and Eve, thanks to the 'Eurocentric' interpretation of the Adamic myth). Christendom, Europe, 'Europeanizes' the Hebrews and Jews, the Greeks and the Romans, the primitive Christians and even the Byzantines.[4]

The reality is the opposite. The neolithic revolution, which began in Mesopotamia with the organization of confederations of cities in the fourth millenium, in Egypt in the third millenium, some time later in the Indus valley (modern Pakistan), later in China, and later moved east, crossing the Pacific Ocean and, through the influence of Polynesian and other east Asian cultures, reached the New World. The classical culture of Teotihuacán in the valley of Mexico flourished from AD 400 to 800, and Tiahuacano beside Lake Titicaca in Bolivia a little earlier. It was a gigantic 'march to the west'. The inhabitants of the New World were part of the Far East, Asian in their roots, languages and religions.

In 1492 the Europe of Christendom, from Vienna (besieged a little earlier by the Turks) to Seville (near which in January of that year the last crusade of Christendom recovered Granada from the hands of Muslims in Europe), with something less than sixty million people after the population disaster of the fourteenth century (perhaps three to four times fewer than inhabited the territory of the Chinese empire at the time), occupied a tiny eastern corner of the map, largely dominated by the Muslim world, the vast Dar-el-Islam. From Morocco the Moslem world stretched south across the Sahara, reached modern Tunis, Egypt, the caliphate of Baghdad, the kingdoms of Iran, the Moghul empire (a little later), the trading sultanates of Malacca and Indochina, and as far as the island of Mindanao in the southern Philippines. The only real ecumenical universality in the fifteenth century was Muslim: from the Atlantic to the Pacific, from the Mongol khanates, defeated only a short time before by the principality of Moscow, to the kingdoms of the African savannah. European, Latin–German Christendom was 'peripheral' – and had never been 'central' in world history.

By means of the crusades (in part a product of the European demographic expansion which resulted from the great agricultural revolution of the tenth century onwards),[5] the Europe of Christendom had attempted to conquer the centre of the contemporary world market, Palestine and Egypt, the meeting point of the Mediterranean (which was not a Christian sea until after the battle of Lepanto in 1571) and the 'Arab Sea' (later the 'Indian Ocean'). The merchants of Venice, Amalfi, Naples, Genoa and Barcelona helped with the crusades for the recovery of the Holy Sepulchre (a motive even naively suggested by St Bernard), but were in reality an instrument of an economic and political expansionist project of the trading powers of Christendom in the Mediterranean. The Muslims repulsed all these crusades, and the Europe of Christendom continued to be 'shut in' on itself and 'peripheral'.

1.2 The 'expansion' of Europe: the conquest of the New World

There is nothing surprising in the fact that it should have been at its extremities that the Europe of Christendom was able to evade the blockade maintained for centuries by the Muslim world. The principality of Moscow, the Third Rome, expanded east, across the tundra, and was to reach the Pacific at the beginning of the seventeenth century. The Czarist empire was to guarantee the Orthodox world ('Oriental', not strictly 'European') the presence of Christianity in north Asia.

Portugal, too, from the end of the fourteenth century, and decisively from 1413, when it captured the North African port of Ceuta from the Muslims, began the expansion of 'European' Christendom. Compared with this phenomenon, the Renaissance, the Reformation and even the

Enlightenment are internal European events, but not world events. 1492 is the first 'European' date in world history, and from this point the 'centrality' of Europe was slowly constructed in the sixteenth century. The process was begun by Portugal and Spain, which were later tossed to one side and exploited as 'semi-peripheral' by 'central' Europe, Holland, France, England, Germany, principally from the Industrial Revolution of the eighteenth century, though from much earlier by the financial power of the European bankers.[6]

The so-called 'conquest' of America, carried out mainly by Hispanic Christendom, has to be placed in the context of this other European 'expansion', more specifically, from the Mediterranean, starting-point of the navigators, source of much of the financial resources and origin of the conflicts of interest with the Muslim world of the eastern Mediterranean). In reality, at the beginning the Atlantic was an eastern branch of the Mediterranean, until Columbus' second voyage in 1493; from that date the Mediterranean became a secondary eastern branch of the Atlantic, and its 'centrality' died with that of the Muslim world at Lepanto, a victory for the Hispanic gold and silver won in the New World, with the blood of Indians and black African slaves.

The expansion of European Christendom, Luso–Hispanic at the beginning, took place under the mercantile system. Trade with the Muslim world was partly replaced by the Portuguese, who impoverished the Muslim world with the precious metals of the New World (through a process of inflation which drained the Muslim world's money of its value). This trade was enormously expanded by Spain, which opened up new markets and products which could be traded in them. Mercantilism transferred to Europe huge quantities of 'money' (gold and silver), which came through Spain, first via Seville and later through Cadiz and was deposited in the chests of the bankers in Genoa, Augsburg or Amsterdam and, with the passage of time, in London. Spain was able to acquire 'money' but, having destroyed its nascent bourgeoisie (Jews, Moors, communards, etc.), was unable to transform it into 'capital'.[7]

1.3 The 'actors' in the conquest

The actors in the process of domination involved in the conquest were, to name but a few, 'money capital',[8] the state (in Spain and the 'state' of the Indies), the conquistadores, the missionaries and those who suffered the consequences (the 'object' of the domination). Their praxes intersected in all directions, though the 'social relations' had different directions and therefore different meanings.[9] Each one of these 'actors' had a different function, and it should be borne in mind that there were also differences between each one of these classes or fractions of classes. The first four constituted the hegemonic 'historic bloc' in power, and the fifth the origin of the 'social bloc', the oppressed, the Latin American 'people'.[10]

The Five 'Actors' in the Conquest (before 1530)

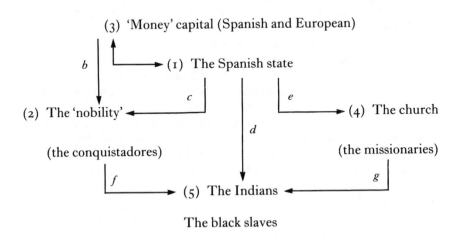

Numbers in brackets indicate the 'actors'; the arrows (*a, b*, etc.) the 'social relations'. The direction of the arrow (→) indicates the practice of domination; the opposite direction is the practice of the subjugated.

The Crown, their Hispanic Majesties (with the union of Aragon and Castile in 1479), the emerging Spanish state (which was at the same time the 'State of the Indies' [1]), controlled by its 'lordship' the whole structure of the conquest (arrows *c, d* and *e*):

God our Lord has deigned to give us the Lordship of this world . . .[11]

Without a shadow of a doubt, it was the dominant 'actor'.

In second place came the Spanish 'nobility' (2), with its 'fractions': the 'grandees', large landowners who controlled the agricultural and pastoral system of the *mesta*, the sheep-breeders' union; those who possessed titles, the knights (*caballeros*) and lastly the squires (*hidalgos*), ninety per cent of the nobility. They were the main, though not the only, military 'actors' of the conquest. They were the mainstay of the monarchy, its privileged subjects (arrow *c*). The crisis of agriculture and livestock raising, the depopulation of Spain, sent them off to the Indies as 'conquerors'.

Thirdly (3) the merchants (at the beginning of the Hispanic Mediterranean), the possessors of money in Spain (Andalucia or Castile), who paid or lent money for the ventures of the conquest, and who, very soon, came to be dependent on the big foreign financiers of Central Europe (the Fuggers, the Welzers, the Eingers, the Sayllers, etc.). They had enormous power, even over the monarchy (arrow *a*) and the nobility (*b*). The Spanish bourgeoisie was weak, as a result of the expulsion of the Jews and the Moors, and the defeat of the communards in the wars of 1519 to 1521, when Charles V, influenced by advisers controlled by Flemish finance capital, finally destroyed the possibility of the emergence of a Spanish 'bourgeoisie'. This weakness was to determine the fate of the Hispanic and Latin American world for the next five centuries. To these groups must be added the merchants or traders, mine-owners and slave-owning estate or plantation owners who appeared later in the Indies.

In fourth place there was the church (4), which held a third of all land in Spain, and was the third power of the kingdom, after the Crown and the nobility. With its plentiful clergy, its powerful bishops and archbishops (men to be feared even in the military sphere), its cultural power in the universities, the church pervaded both public and everyday life. However, by a well-organized system of patronage, Christendom had at its head the King (arrow *e*). Rome was in the background, but the patronage system allowed no direct intervention of the Pope in the New World (until after the wars of emancipation, from 1826 onwards). Missionaries performed an essential function in the conquest.

The whole made up Hispanic Christendom (parallel, with a few differences, to that of Portugal), which threw itself into the activity of the 'Conquest' as an immediate continuation of the 'Reconquest': the one ended in January 1492 and the other began in October of the same year.

The fifth actor (5), this time from the New World, the Indians and later the black slaves, was to be the base of the pyramid of power, the dominated, 99% of the population by the end of the sixteenth century (if we include the various categories of mixed-race persons, white-Indian, white-African, mulatto-Indian and creole). All the arrows of domination (*f*, *d*, and *g*) converge on them. They are the 'other'. The poor.[12]

II. The 'motives' of the conquest

It has to be understood, from the outset and as a general premise, that the fundamental 'motive' was the fulfilment of an 'ideal of Christendom' which, however, was by now no longer feudal or medieval, but renaissance, the first phase of the modern age. Nevertheless, the 'motives' had not yet separated out. The complex of political, economic, and cultural-religious motives presents itself as an indivisible structure. And yet, because we are in the first phase of the modern period, it is already an emerging mercantile, money capitalist world. 'Wealth' is gold, not yet industrial capital in the strict sense. According to Bartolomé de Las Casas,

> Their reason for killing and destroying such an infinite number of souls is that the Christians have an ultimate aim, which is to acquire gold, and to swell themselves with riches in a very brief time and thus *rise to high estate disproportionate to their merits*.[13]

This passage shows very clearly the parallel motivations (causes), wealth (gold, the 'money' of mercantilism) and the 'honour' sought by the 'squires' (or those who claim to be such 'disproportionate to their merits'). It is not, as in the case of the Dutch and English East and West India Companies, an essential capitalist motivation. It is something older and therefore not in contradiction with the 'ideal of Christendom' in the Reconquest from the Muslims, in which defending the faith, winning honour and acquiring wealth were simultaneous motivations.

This position needs to be distinguished from two 'legends'. It is different from the 'black legend', invented in the Low Countries in their struggle against Spain at the beginning of the seventeenth century and later used by England in its fight for world domination – the English used Las Casas to criticize the process of the conquest, even though their aims were the same and their methods no less unjust. And clearly it is not the 'Hispanicist legend', which grew up after 1930 in Francoism and Latin American populism, and in Catholic conservatism (for example Josef Hoeffner), in which the actions of Spain, of Catholicism, are defended and the genocide and subsequent final and unjust subjugation of the indigenous peoples are totally ignored. The Hispanicists had to refute Bartolomé de Las Casas, and their apologists set out to do so. The position which begins with Las Casas is different. It is the position of Latin American critical thought and theology. This, after weighing all the factors, comes to adopt the position of the indigenous, the black slave, the creole, the oppressed and the poor, as the position which follows from the gospel.

2.1 'The Lordship of this world'[14]

First the practical motive of political domination justifies the destruction of the military defences – if any exist – of the former sovereign power. This is the action of the state (of the Crown and the 'State of the Indies', embodied from 1524 in the Council of the Indies). Consequently, the 'conquest' is first and foremost a 'war of occupation', preceded by the allegedly innocent 'discovery' and continued by the 'colonization' or 'exploitation' in the strict sense:

I beseech your Majesty, even though my insistence may be ill-timed, not to grant or allow what the tyrants have devised, carried forward and committed, *what they call conquest* . . .[15] Let it not be granted to them, or it will be a violation of natural and divine law, and bring as a result most serious mortal sins, deserving of terrible and eternal torments . . . Rather [let your Majesty] cover this infernal demand with eternal silence.[16]

Planting the cross on an island, on a beach, in a village, in the square of Aztec Mexico or Inca Cuzco, is an act of 'dominion', of possession; it proclaims the sovereignty of the Spanish state in the person of the King. It is a 'social relation' of domination. This 'relation' is a sin, the fundamental, structural sin. This 'motive' was to be the basis of European expansion for the last half-millenium. It is the fundamental *theological fact* of the whole modern period – and the post-moderns are no less 'Eurocentric', a Heidegger or a Nietzsche, beginning not only with the Cartesian *ego cogito*, but with the royal *ego conquiro* mediated by the physical, empirical *conquistador*, Hernán Cortés or Pizarro: 'will to power' over 'the other'.[17]

The first 'actor' (1) exercises dominion over all the others (in the diagram [2], [4] and [5], and relatively over [3]). Obviously this practical position is based on a 'theology of Christendom', of the expansion of Western Christian culture over the Muslims, the pagans, who die without salvation in their perversions and witchcraft.

2.2 'To swell themselves with riches in a very brief time'

This is the aspect which has rightly been stressed, though I have tried to show that, while it (materially) determines the political factor, it is also (practically) determined by it.[18]

Here the 'motives' followed by three 'actors' come into full play: practical realization by the *conquistador* (2), who is supported by the power of the absolute monarchy (1), and the ultimate beneficiary, mercantile-financial capital, in Spain and Portugal and finally in Italy, the Netherlands, Germany and England (3). It is the 'productive-economic' conquest, of precious metals, money, and tropical products, so valuable because they express, as luxuries, the emerging power of the European bourgeoisies.

These motivations can be seen very clearly in the protagonists of the 'discovery', who anticipate the protagonists of the 'conquest'. In the contract of 17 April 1492 the Crown expressed them to Christopher Columbus, in a text which he helped to draft, to ensure that none of his prerogatives should be left out:

Your Highnesses, being Lords of the said ocean seas, guarantee to the said Don Christopher Columbus . . . that all and any goods, whether pearls, precious stones, gold, silver, spices and any other things and merchandise of whatever sort, number and manner, which may be bought, bartered, obtained by chance, won or had within the boundaries of the said Admiralty . . .[19]

It is interesting to note the detail Columbus insists on with regard to the possibilities of new 'riches' which might be found. There is no end to the familiar examples – something I have investigated in detail in some of my books[20] – which show how the *conquistadores* sought nothing more than gold, pearls, riches:

A cacique . . . called Hatuey . . . said to them, 'Now you must know that they are saying that the Christians are coming here . . . because they have a God they greatly worship . . . You see their God here.' . . . He had a basket full of gold and jewels and said, 'You see their God here, the God of the Christians. See here, if we keep this basket of gold, they will take it from us and will end up by killing us. So let us cast away the basket into the river.'[21]

At the beginning it was the gold to be found in the rivers. But by 1520 there was no more gold on Santo Domingo. Then began the cultivation of sugar, black slavery. The *encomienda*, or allocation of indigenous serfs, gave way to *haciendas*, estates (for agricultural exploitation); the *mita*, labour assigned for mining; and plantations (for the exploitation of tropical produce). The indigenous, and later the black slaves, were the 'hands' (in a 'social relation of production') exploited by the dominators (the practical political level of domination is now connected with production involving nature, the economic, practical production level).[22]

The theologies of Juan Ginés de Sepúlveda (in Spain) or Fr Antonio Vieira (in Brazil) are real 'theologies of domination' – they justify the subjugation of the Indians, the slaves, and regard the 'conquest' and 'slavery' as 'civilizing' – today we would say 'modern' – processes. It needs to be understood that this theology justifies the motivations of the 'conquistadores' (2) and comes into contradiction with the interests of the Crown (1). From the beginning of the sixteenth century the Crown had begun to see that the *encomenderos* and Spanish elites in the Indies were reducing the power of the King in these territories, and as a result the prophetic missionaries (4) had space to criticize these claims to domination and possession of slaves – with the support of the Crown.

2.3 'God our Lord . . . has been pleased to grant us . . . the Lordship of this world'[23]

By the papal bulls *Aeterni Regis* of 1455 for Portugal and *Inter coetera* of

1493 for Spain, the church was turned into an *internal* component of the power structure of the Crown, of the 'Christendom of the Indies' under the absolute control of the 'Council of the Indies'. These bulls began the Roman Pope's handover of the Latin American church to the Spanish state, and subsequently to the United States, as when Texas, New Mexico and California were stolen from Mexico in 1848, or when Puerto Rico, Cuba and the Philippines attained emancipation from Spain in 1898.[24] The 'Laws of the Kingdoms of the Indies' are an ecclesiastical and a civil code at the same time. Evangelization is a power and a responsibility of the monarchy, although the church (4) is the direct agent of the mission, the '*spiritual* conquest', as Robert Ricard called it, not noticing the contradiction in terms between 'conquest' and 'evangelization',[25] an issue which Las Casas dealt with in his *Del único modo* (1538), when he sought to demonstrate the need for evangelization to exclude violence.[26]

Columbus had already expressed this motivation in his diary of his first voyage in 1492:

> Your Highnesses, as Catholics, Christians and Princes who love the holy Christian faith and wish to see it increase, and are enemies of the sect of Mahomet and all idolatries and heresies, have seen fit to send me, Christopher Columbus, to the said parts of the Indies to see . . . what way there may be to convert them to our holy faith.[27]

If religion was 'the foundation of the state' (Hegel),[28] the religious motivation of the evangelization of the Indians became, as might be expected, the justification for the conquest. In the end it was the only rational case which could be made. Thus the enterprise of domination was left fetishized, and the 'gold of the Indies' became a 'god', in the words of the Dominican from sixteenth-century Bolivia which stand at the head of this article: 'whom the Spaniards' greed sacrifices to their God'. There is perfect theological articulation between the mining economy and idolatry: gold and silver are transformed into a 'god' of death. The evangelization performed by the church (4) justified the action of the political power (1), of economic power (of [2] and [3]) and gave the church itself absolute control over culture (education, the level of ideology and customs). The indigenous peoples and the black slaves were *absolutely* denied as historico-cultural subjects with their own rights.

On the other hand, it cannot be denied that many missionaries and Christians evangelized in simplicity and poverty, distinguishing between the church and oppressive Spanish society, but they were never hegemonic: they never had control of the whole church. They had it in certain periods in certain regions, thanks to certain individuals, but the 'structure' of power remained located always in the 'Council of the Indies' and the subordinates of the Patronate as an organ of Christendom. The Jesuits, for example, would not admit the power of the Council of the Indies in their missions, and in time this became one of the reasons for their expulsion, from Brazil in 1759 and from Spanish America in 1767. Their expulsion, together with the ancient expulsions of Jews, Moors and communards in the sixteenth century, denied Latin America any possibility of starting the industrial revolution in the eighteenth century.

2.4 The prophetic critique of idolatrous motivations

From 1510, with the voice of Antón de Montesinos in Hispaniola (modern Dominican Republic and Haiti), a group of Dominicans launched a critique of the 'social relation' of domination over the Indians known as the *encomienda* (Indians were required to work for nothing for a Spanish master for a certain time). This was the exploitation which Bartolomé de Las Casas exposed clearly in 1514 at the moment of his 'conversion'.[29]

There was a prophetic generation. Between 1504 and 1620 33% of the bishops were Dominicans and *lascasianos*, and some of them were martyred, like Antonio de Validivieso in Nicaragua, and others expelled, including Pablo de Torres in Panama.[30] They were able to 'discern' the motives of the various protagonists of the conquest. Among the thousands of documentary testimonies I have copied and published is this one, from Bishop Juan Ramírez of Guatemala, referring to the indigenous women:

> The sixth form of force and violence never heard of in other nations and kingdoms is that women are forced against their will, the married women against the wishes of their husbands, the unmarried women and girls of ten or fifteen years against the wishes of their fathers and mothers . . . They are taken from their homes and forced to serve others, *encomenderos* in other persons. . . , in the course of which they are often made to be prostitutes for the master of the house, for men of mixed race or mulattos or blacks . . .[31]

Some missionaries and bishops, exclusively members of the church and not servants of the state, were able to perform this prophetic function. They were, however, a minority, at some moments dominant, as when their influence secured the appointment of the Hieronymites at the beginning of the conquest of Santo Domingo, or the promulgation of the 'New Laws' in 1542 (though in both cases they ultimately failed), but never victorious. They were defeated by the Spanish or creole ruling class in power from 1492 until today, despite changes in these classes or class fractions during the long history of five centuries of domination. In the process of emancipation (from 1809 onwards) or since the Second Vatican Council (with Medellín in 1968) this prophetic tradition was to enjoy a resurgence, and a temporary dominance, only subsequently to be defeated once more.[32]

Some members of this prophetic tradition, at the time (4), criticized the *conquistadores* (2), relying on the power of the King (1)[33] – since at the time it was good tactics to fight for the distant sovereign in order to overcome the nearby oppressors of the Indians, though without being able to escape the rule of 'gold' (3), whose idolatrous rule pervaded all. For them the main motive of the conquest was:

> their insatiable greed and ambition, the greatest ever seen in the world. And also, those lands are so rich and felicitous, the native peoples so meek and patient . . . that our Spaniards have no more consideration for them than beasts . . . But I should not say 'than beasts', for, thanks be to God, they have treated beasts with some respect; I should say instead like excrement on the public squares.[34]

It was the beginning of modern times – in relation to which many today claim to be 'post-moderns' – of capitalism, in which the New World was established as a mediation of exploitability (nature was a mediation of wealth) and domination (other people, 'the other', was also a mediation sacrificed to the new 'god': Gold, Money, Moloch).

2.5 The discoverers of the 'real' motives

There were protagonists, 'objects' of the conquest, who discovered with their own eyes, the eyes of the 'other', the eyes of the poor, their eyes clear-sighted because they were totally outside the system which was beginning to be established (and which in 1992 will celebrate a triumphant half-millenium of exploiting the peripheral New Worlds of the South), the 'meaning' and the 'real' motives of the actions of the European *conquistadores*. These were the Indians and later the black African slaves. I will quote only one text from a prophecy of Chilam Balam de Chumayel from the Maya of Mesoamerica, in the *Libro de los Linajes*:

> In the Eleventh Ahau there begins the counting of the time . . .
> It was only because of the mad time, the mad priests, that sadness came among us, that Christianity came among us; for the great Christians came here with the true God; but that was the beginning of our distress, the beginning of the tribute, the beginning of the alms, what made the hidden discord appear,
> the beginning of the fighting with firearms,
> the beginning of the outrages,

the beginning of being stripped of everything,
the beginning of slavery for debts,
the beginning of the debts bound to the shoulders,
the beginning of the constant quarrelling,
the beginning of the suffering.
It was the beginning of the work of the Spaniards and the priests . . .[35]

The Indians were outsiders, outside the Spanish 'community of communication' (to use Habermas' language); they did not participate in that community, they were excluded. Fernández de Oviedo even said that 'they had become bestial because of their customs', which meant that, 'though rational', they did not count as such. But because they were outside they were able to see the actions of the Europeans (in what the 'invaders' thought of as the 'New' World, but what was for the Indians the world of always), and interpret it hermeneutically with an extreme clarity. It was the poor, to whom the 'kingdom of the heavens' belongs, the 'pure of heart', who exposed the 'motives' which have produced the suffering in their wretched, tortured, starved bodies, from 1492 to 1992, and will do so for a long time to come.

From the point of view of the Indians (5), 'discovery' and 'conquest' were a single movement, an 'invasion'. It was the 'invasion' of 'our' world (for the Europeans 'America'), which became 'theirs', as the indigenous inhabitants became the 'excluded'. From this perspective their land had been occupied by the whole panoply of 'actors': the *conquistador* (2) with his lust for wealth, honour and the glory of a 'squire' (*hidalgo*, 'son of someone', when in reality they were very often sons of nobodies), the church (4), which claimed to evangelize but (except for the prophets) could do nothing but justify the 'conquest', the King (1), who, though unknown because so distant, was feared as an almighty foreign god, and much more invisible to their eyes, the bankers of Genoa and Augsburg, the real 'invisible gods', fetishes. All these had occupied their lands, stolen their women (and slept with them) and children (and brought them up in an alien culture) – the end of a world. It is true that God performed a miracle of the Spirit among them and they became Christians, in the face of so many scandals, but that is not the subject of this article.

I should like to end by pointing out that now that the Berlin Wall – which separated West and East – has 'fallen', we need to consider, with a view to destroying it too, a wall immensely higher and longer, which divides the rich capitalist countries from the poor *capitalist* and 'free market' countries. The North–South wall should now be our concern, and it should be remembered that its building began, not in the 1960s, but in 1492, and its triumphant effectiveness is to be celebrated in 1992, rendering invisible, in everyday ideology and dominant theology, the wretched countries of the South.

Translated by Francis McDonagh

Notes

1. See my articles 'La cristiandad moderna ante el otro', *Concilium* 150, 1979, pp. 498–506; 'Was America discovered or invaded,', *Concilium* 200, 1988, 126–34. For further discussion see my books, *A History of the Church in Latin America: Colonization to Liberation (1492–1979)*, Grand Rapids, Mi. 1981; *Les évêques hispano-américains, défenseurs et évangélisateurs de l'indien (1504–1620)*, Wiesbaden 1970, bibliography, pp. XXI–LXI; *Desintegración de la Cristiandad y liberación*, Salamanca 1978. With particular reference to the work of Fernando Mires, *En nombre de la cruz. Discusiones teológicas y políticas frente al holocausto de los indios*, San José 1986; background documents in Eberhard Schmitt (ed.), *Die grossen Entdeckungen*, Vol. II, Munich 1982.

2. See my exposition in IAMS (Rome): 'Future of Mission in the Third Millennium', in *Mission Studies* (Aachen) V 2, 1988, 66–89 (also in 'Towards a History of the Church in the World Periphery', in: *Towards a History of the Church in the Third World*, EATWOT working commission, Berne 1983.

3. For Hegel everything starts with the 'oriental world', *Philosophie der Geschichte*, Teil I, *Werke*, Vol. 12, Frankfurt, pp. 142ff., the 'Greek world' (ibid., pp. 275ff.), etc, or in 'World history' (*Rechtsphilosophie, Werke*, Vol 7, pp. 509ff.). For more details on the idea of the world history of 'east–west' (in Europe) and the 'west–east' necessary to explain the history of the present Third World, see my *Historia General de la Iglesia en América Latina*, vol. I, 'Introduction', Salamanca 1983, pp. 1–100; and also in the chapter 'La Histórica Latinoamericana', in *Filosofía ética latinoamericana* (1973), Mexico 1977, pp. 27ff. (Buenos Aires ²1988).

4. Samir Amin, *Eurocentrism*, Monthly Review, New York 1989, an Arab view, still Mediterranean, but very useful.

5. See Cherubini Giovanni, *Agricoltura e societa rurales nel medioevo*, Florence 1972; Georges Duby, *L'économie rurale et la vie des campagnes dans l'Occident médiéval*, Vols. I–II, Paris 1962, etc. From 1000 to 1340 the population of Europe rose from twenty-four million to something over fifty million.

6. See I. Wallerstein, *The Modern World-System*, Vols. I–II, New York 1974–80; Maurice Dobb, *Studies in the Development of Capitalism*, London 1946.

7. This inability to transform money into capital explains the early poverty of Spain, from the end of the sixteenth century – the beginning of the growth, first of the Low Countries and later of England's Cromwell, at the height of the seventeenth century. Marx describes perfectly this transformation of money into capital (see *Capital* I, Chap. 4, MEGA II, b, pp. 128–61). See my books *La producción teórica de Marx*, Mexico 1985, Chap. 7, 'Hacia un Max desconocido', ibid., 1988; Ch. 3: 'El Marx definitivo (1863–1882)'; ibid., 1990, Chs. 2 and 5.

8. 'Money', not yet mediated by the 'subsumption' of 'living labour' as wage labour in the process of production, can be considered as the first 'determination' of capital, but not in the strict sense, that is, as '*industrial* capital'. See my writings cited in n. 7 above. Spain therefore participated in the 'primitive accumulation' of the 'treasure-money'

which appeared in mercantile circulation: the New World gave the initial 'loan', without any interest, to the nascent modern capitalist Europe.

9. See the theological sense of *'social'* (not 'communal') relation in my book *Ethics and Community*, Chapters 2–3 and 11–12: as sin (praxis), structural, institutional and historical determination.

10. For a synopsis see Ciro Cardoso and Hector Pérez Brignoli, *Historia Económica de América Latina*, Editorial Crítica, Barcelona Vol. I, 1979, for this topic, esp. pp. 108–211.

11. First title, first law of the first book of the *Leyes de los Reynos de las Indias* (recompiled in 1681), Madrid 1943, vols I–II.

12. On the 'other' as poor, applying to the process of the conquest E. Levinas' category of 'exteriority', see my book *Para una ética de la liberación latinoamericana*, vols. I–II, Buenos Aires 1973, Vol. III; Mexico 1977. T. Todorov and others, *The Conquest of America*, New York 1985, have drawn on the ideas of this book without acknowledging it.

13. Bartolomé de Las Casas, *The Devastation of the Indies. A Brief Account*, New York 1974, p. 41 (emphasis added).

14. From the first title of the first law of Book 1 of the *Leyes de los Reynos de las Indias*; see above, note 11.

15. Bartolomé de Las Casas, *Brevísima relación de la destrucción de las Indias*, Buenos Aires 1966, p. 30 (this passage does not appear in the English version cited in note 13 – *Translator*).

16. Las Casas, *Brevísima relación*, p. 31.

17. See again my *Ethics and Community*, Chapters 2ff.

18. Marx notes that 'production' may be determined by 'distribution' (the practical factor): 'A conquering people [*eroberndes Volk*] divides the land among the conquerors, thus imposes a certain distribution and form of property in land, and thus determines production' (*Grundrisse*, Introduction, Penguin Books and New Left Review, London 1973, p. 96). In this case the practical political level determines the productive economic level. Marx was not an economist, and did not put forward a 'productivist paradigm', as Jürgen Habermas believes (see, e.g., *Die philosophische Diskurs der Moderne*, Frankfurt 1985, 'Exkurs' to the third lecture).

19. Quoted in I. P. Maguidovich, *Historia del descubrimiento y exploración de Latinoamérica*, Moscow n.d., p. 31.

20. For example, in my nine volumes on *El episcopado latinoamericano defensor del indio (1504–1620)*, Cuernavaca 1969–71, which reproduce (from the unpublished sources of the Archivo General de Indias [Seville]) hundreds of testimonies to this gold fever which shone in the eyes of the *'conquistadores'*, which scandalized some missionaries, and was the cause of the 'devastation of the Indies' and of the genocide without parallel which opened the famous modern period.

21. Bartolomé de Las Casas, *Devastation*, pp. 54–5. Marx quotes this text, without knowing it is from Las Casas, when he writes: 'The Cuban natives regarded gold as the Spaniards' fetish. They celebrated a feast in its honour . . . Those savages would have regarded firewood as the Rhinelanders' fetish' ('The law abut thefts of firewood', Marx, *Obras fundamentales*, Mexico 1982, p. 283 = MEW 1, p. 147, translated from the Spanish).

22. See my *Philosophy of Liberation*, Maryknoll 1985, for a critique of Habermas' ignorance of the 'practical productive' level (neither merely practical nor merely productive or productivist; that is, neither merely practical political reason nor instrumental reason, but 'economic reason', real, practical-productive, a different type

of 'rationality'). In theology it is 'sacramental (eucharistic) reason'. The 'economic' or 'eucharistic' level (see my *Herrschaft und Befreiung*, Freiburg 1985) is not clearly brought out by theology influenced by Habermas (see Edmund Arens, *Habermas und die Theologie*, Patmos, Düsseldorf 1989). Even Helmut Peukert's study, pp. 39–64, does not succeed in grasping the concrete and synthetic level of the economic, and this is not surprising, because Habermas left 'economics' as a 'system' juxtaposed to the 'life-world' and did not see its essential role. See also Helmut Peukert, *Science, Action and Fundamental Theology. Toward a Theology of Communicative Action*, Massachusetts 1986; see also my essay, 'La Introducción de la *Transformación de la Filosofía* de K. O. Apel y la Filosofía de la Liberación', Freiburg dialogue of 24 November 1989, to be published in *Argument*, Hamburg 1990. Certainly liberation theology will have to begin again the constructive dialogue (with a critical edge based on the eucharistic-economic 'desperate poverty' of the Third World's 'hunger without bread') with the theology of the Habermas school, just as at the end of the 1960s there was a dialogue with the theologies based on the work of Ernst Bloch or the Frankfurt School of the period. The 'Eurocentrism' and 'developmentalism' of Popper's or Max Weber's 'open society' is much more influential in this theology than these authors think: there is a need for a new North–South dialogue. The 'other', the outsider to the 'community of communication' (such as the person who does not argue because they do not form part of that 'community'), has been excluded, but they have previously been 'excluded' from participation in the 'bread' (because they are the 'poor person' whom John Rawls is unable to situate in his formal discourse).

23. From the text cited in note 14 above.

24. See my article, 'Vatican Policy in Latin America', to be published shortly in *Social Compass* (Brussels).

25. This was the theme of my lecture in El Escorial, 'Historia de la fe cristiana y cambio social en América Latina', in: *Fe cristiana y cambio social en América Latina*, Salamanca 1973, pp. 65–100.

26. *Del único modo de atraer a todos los pueblos a la verdadera religión*, Mexico 1975 – a perfect example of an '*ideal* community of discussion' (as defined by Karl O. Apel, *Transformation der Philosophie*, 2 vols, Frankfurt 1973).

27. *Diario*, II Parte, Madrid 1977, p.28.

28. See Hegel, *Philosophie der Religion*, I, C, III (*Werke*, ed. cited in note 3 above, vol. 16, pp. 236–7).

29. I have described the details of his prophetic 'conversion' in my Introduction to vol. I of the *Historia general de la Iglesia en América Latina*, pp. 17–24. In the text of Ecclesiasticus/Sirach 34.18ff. Bartolomé relates the eucharist to economic structures (see my 'The Bread of the Eucharistic Celebration as a Sign of Justice in the Community', *Concilium* 152, 1982, 56–65. As early as 1964 I mentioned this text, which is central to the history of the New World prophetic tradition (*Esprit* [Paris], July 1965, pp. 53–65).

30. See my *El episcopado latinoamericano y la liberación de los pobres (1504–1620)*, Mexico 1979.

31. *Archivo General de Indias*, Guatemala 156, 10 March 1603 (which may be consulted along with seventeen other injustices in my book cited in note 30 above, pp. 89–95). This subject is the theme of Chapter VII, 'La erótica latinoamericana', of my *Para una ética de la liberación latinoamericana*, Vol. III, Mexico 1977.

32. On these three phases of prophecy, see my study of this history of Latin American theology, *Prophetie und Kritik*, Freiburg 1989 (shortly to appear in English).

33. See Enrique Semo, *Historia del capitalismo en México. Los orígenes (1521–1763)*, Mexico 1976.

34. Bartolomé de Las Casas, *The Devastation of the Indies*, pp. 41–2.

35. In: Miguel León-Portilla, *El reverso de la conquista*, Mexico 1978, p. 86. See also Nathan Wachtel, *La vision des vaincus*, Paris 1971; Tzvetan Todorov and Georges Baudot, *Racconti Aztechi della conquista*, Turin 1988.

Present Consequences of the European Invasion of America

Aiban Wagua

A history in their terms, and for them not us

'Five centuries have had to go by before these men have taken any notice of our values, but this experience shows us that we have always been deceived. Although at present we are under their roof, as friends, may they not be hiding something up their sleeve? Are they sincere? Historically we know that there are dead people who do not die and living people who now are dead.'[1] The history told us by our elders is of these dead who do not die and living people who are dead now. This is living history, assaulted, silenced, marginalized but still resisting. It is our history, and we try to nourish ourselves from it. In it the events of half a millennium take on very particular and painful names that we can feel and place:

We are marginalized and they (the whites) want to wipe us off the earth.[2]

Governments deceive us, exploit us, talk nonsense to us.[3]

We are the real owners of this our mother land, we were the first, our grandparents were the first to drink from these rivers and lay their bones in this mother, and now they tell us they are giving it to us, that we have to ask them for laws to allow us to cultivate it, that they are the owners.[4]

They (the whites) tell us they have brought us a god; this is a lie, they have brought us many gods, they muddled everything up, they closed the way to us.[5]

Indigenous cultures, indigenous religions, indigenous men and women . . . are elements of resistance. We have been waging a long and painful war for the last five hundred years. Millions of our brothers and sisters have fallen in it, many others have taken refuge in inhospitable regions of our mother land, and many prefer to accept the foreigners' impositions in order to survive . . . Our elders are restrained when they evoke the tales of the European invasion, but their faces become flushed and angry when they take us by the hand to look at our history today. They remind us that we should not ask them to dwell on the blood that was shed, the places that bore witness, the Spaniards with guns, but realize that we are landless today, that we are living today in this position, in this trench, facing these enemies. Our grandparents know many stories of the European invasion, but it means much more to them when these stories are put in the present bloody context of our communities; they set fire to the trunk, and the tree is still painfully burning. This is the view of our native history we take in this article. We shall try to order and synthesize the main ideas we shared at our indigenous meetings for Abia Yala,[6] in particular between 1986 to 1989.

Here it is important to clarify the church's historical role. At our indigenous meetings we find it difficult to sort out the church's place in our problems. Certainly the church was responsible for desecrating and eliminating our religions; without knowing anything about them, she condemned them as superstitions, works of the devil, satanic. But it is also undeniable that the church played a part in protecting our fathers from the teeth of greedy invaders. Often the church justified the cultural, religious, even physical death of our fathers, our communities, and at other times she tried to save them and defend them. The church's role has been ambiguous, divided, and continues to be so. It has been a question of catholic churches, rather than the Catholic church. The theoretical pastoral directives of the church relating to our communities have nearly always been clear, but there has been division in carrying them out, even fighting. We should be well aware of these complexities when we speak about the church and the indigenous problem.

The 'indigenous problem' itself also has its complexities. There are some fairly common problems at the level of our communities, but it is very important to analyse them in their different contexts. There are indigenous problems, rather than an indigenous problem, indigenous needs, indigenous demands . . . but without forgetting solidarity. 'An Indian alone is a dead Indian' as our fathers used to say.

Socio-political and economic consequences

We have to cope with two histories. They contradict each other and are opposed. One is *uaga*[7] history and the other indigenous. *Uaga* history is a past history, of something that happened in the past, bloodshed, gospel-preaching that was misunderstood, the extirpation of idolatries practised at the church's obscurantist stage, the colonists and agents of the Spanish crown who attacked the Indians . . . And those who control that history tell us that it is very bad taste to keep harping so much on the past, because 'things have changed'. This is history told by those who invaded us, *uaga* history. But it is not the only history, or the best or the most exact. Our indigenous history is not that of the conquered but of those of us who resisted their death plans for five hundred years. It is a present history, history that is not over but still going on, a living history of oppression and resistance. Our elders tell us of the arrow stuck in the roof that still drips with blood, Indians hacked to death by machetes for defending their crops against the big landlords, the government's failure to demarcate our lands, the buying and selling of Indians in political games, rulers mocking at indigenous demands, rulers' 'legal' complicity in the extermination of our communities . . . For the Indian, just speaking of the invasion five hundred years ago has no meaning: it is absurd, it is not history. It is a way of speaking used by the new invaders to tell us it is all over, we are no longer at war, it is a strategy to maintain their domination. Therefore from the viewpoint of indigenous history the question does not arise of whether or not to celebrate the half millennium of the 'discovery or evangelization of America'. For indigenous history it is a question of whether it is possible or not to celebrate the marginalization, the violence, the genocide or ethnocide perpetrated against our indigenous communities of Abia Yala. We indigenous people know that we can only celebrate our resistance, our indomitable will to go on living in spite of the darkness around us.

In our first indigenous meetings and in view of the quincentenary, we tried to take our elders back to the old stories, and we nearly always concluded that they did not agree about 'history'. Gradually we realized that we were playing on two totally different stages. We were asking our elders about the invaders' view of history, and they were operating from a vision of historical resistance. So in one of our meetings (1988) one Paez leader who had been asked to say something to us about the five hundred years merely took off his shirt and showed us the scars still fresh on his back, and said: 'This is what they have been doing to us for five hundred years!'[9]

From this point of view, and without claiming to give a complete list, we think that the socio-political and economic consquences of the first invasion show up in the following current realities:

Our communities with the most experience of contact with the dominant society are facing a growing flight of our people to the cities, where they create poverty belts together with other marginalized sectors. The causes are very various: boredom with the native communities caused by consumer media, search for paid work, schooling of children, false needs and illusions created by the consumer bombardment, the precariousness of means of subsistence in the indigenous zones . . .

The majority of our indigenous communities have practised agriculture for home consumption, subsistence farming or limited stock-breeding. The exhaustion of moderately usable land – we Indians are confined to the worst lands in Abia Yala – together with the population growth, seriously aggravates the situation. And where production is good, our people find the market sewn up, middlemen protected by the law, exploitation, cheap labour . . .

In political affairs, Latin American countries appear to give 'participation to the Indians' within the general administration. But this is done in a way that not only ignores indigenous administrative structures but even goes against them, causing internal divisions, without leaving any leeway for new and appropriate ways of participation. The indigenous leaders themselves become simple mouthpieces for the rulers' indigenist policies, or merely spokesmen for the political parties they serve, even against the decisions and rights of our indigenous communities.

The education system imposed on us for many years has aimed to quell, tame, civilize, Christianize and whiten indigenous people, and even today its aims are the same. It inculcates the value of everything non-indigenous and detaches us from our roots. From when we are very small we are told that things will go well for us only in *white* terms. They weaken us as persons and disappoint us when we enter their society. As a consequence of the teaching we receive, whose aims are markedly anti-indigenous – and the church has helped maintain this system – we find obstacles put in our way to prevent us getting close to our philosophies, religions, ancestors or deepening our knowledge of them.

Our religions have been abused by Christianity, ridiculed and devalued. Now our religious leaders find it difficult to bring the new generation to the cult of Pachamama, Paba, Wiracocha, Man itu . . . And the invasion of sects is becoming ever more aggressive and corrosive.

Plans made from outside, whether national or ecclesiastical, destroy the integrity of our communities, they open the way to the increasingly harmful entry of the multinationals, who are causing real massacres of our brothers and sisters. They also bring about the increasing militarization of indigenous zones throughout Latin America.

They took away our lands and confined us to the poorest areas, and they continue to take from us the little we still have left. We feel the urgency of laws to defend our rights and genuine self-determination as peoples, nations with our own socio-political, economic and religious systems. And we do not ask this to be granted us out of kindness but as a matter of justice.[9]

Religious consequences

In Latin America the indigenous religions have remained, and in many regions they have become ever more firmly rooted in spite of Christianity. In the name of the gospel, there has been a disgraceful violation of the most delicate, vulnerable and essential part of our cohesion and strength as indigenous communities. This is also part of the history that is not over, which is still going on and causing new problems.

Even the attitude of one sector of the church, which has turned from a pastoral strategy of integration to a more incarnate one of adapting the gospel to our culture, is looked on by some of us with a certain suspicion – is this a new strategy of domination? It is true that this change in the church is due to many factors, but it is still conceived *from outside the indigenous community*, assuming a supposed wish of the indigenous people, in ignorance or non-appreciation of indigenous religions. The official Latin American church still resists, recognizing the indigenous regions as such. Puebla resolves the problem as 'very religious cultures' and opts for the poorest among the poor[10] and not for the *other*. To accepting and recognizing the indigenous religions as capable of giving internal cohesion to our communities in spite of so many death threats would require very radical changes within the church. It would mean an approach based on dialogue between adults; it would mean abandoning the idea of the 'imperfection of the indigenous religions', scattered seeds . . . If of necessity our peoples have to think like the majority in the church, within parameters which are alien to us, how can the church claim to be really universal and what does this make of its equidistance from all cultures?

At the first stage there was much talk of implanting the church, and later it was thought better to create indigenous, native churches. When it was a matter of implanting the church, our brothers and sisters asked in various manifestations of resistance: what church is this? Brought from where? And who has told them we want this church? It took the church five centuries to realize that it was treading on foreign soil and could not implant itself. And now the church tells us that we ourselves are responsible for the new indigenous churches which are to arise. But she knows that we were never prepared for this development. We do not have the timber or the bricks or the straw or the muscles to build our own churches made in our own image and likeness. Do you want *daughters* or sisters? Churches in native dress or native churches?

Some people speak of 'indigenous churches' as a way of continuing to ignore or marginalize the indigenous religions. Others stress practical co-operation in dialogue between religions, or of the large numbers of our brothers and sisters who are indigenous Christians needing a special kind of pastoral care.

It is important for the church to become aware of the generalized movement among the indigenous peoples themselves throughout Latin America to revalue their indigenous religions.[11] With or without recognition by the church, our indigenous religions will continue to resist, survive and grow deeper roots, and this will happen now with greater critical awareness. But if the church does recognize the indigenous religions, this will require pastoral changes:

Not muscling in on the indigenous in anything, opening space for them to carry out their own liberation work.

Confidence in the indigenous people and indigenous culture, even though their criteria, rhythms and actions appear to contradict non-indigenous ways.

We indigenous people must really feel that the church does not think that it is the be-all and end-all of the kingdom of God, its exclusive and perfected instrument.

The church must seek rules, organizations and ways of serving the community through structures which are different from, even opposite to, the 'normal' practice of our non-indigenous fellow Christians.

Recognizing and welcoming without judgment or prejudice from outside the indigenous religions as the normal means of communicating for Paba, Wanaisa, Manitú with their peoples and as sources of resistance and full humanization.

Finally, it must opt not just for the poor, but for the other, for the other who is impoverished. This option must be permeated with clear awareness of the dark role played by the church itself in the history of that other's impoverishment. Therefore collaboration is a matter of justice and not just good will or pity. In taking the indigenous view of history, the church's work cannot be 'with the conquered'. Our elders tell us we have not been conquered yet, that we are still at war, resisting and advancing. In many areas we have advanced and 'conquered part of the church', as our Quechua brother says.[12] Generally the church does not change its position unless it feels seriously threatened.

In this context, the church's pastoral work among our indigenous communities cannot be only raising the fallen, but also opening the way for those of us who are still resisting in a war that has lasted half a millenium, so that this resistance becomes stronger and stronger, victory more real and utopia more aggressive and better understood. For a non-indigenous missionary it means swimming against the tide of his society, free from condescension and continually seeking joint liberation. Not in order to isolate and conserve the indigenous as an archaic relic of humanity, but in support of their total liberation. The mere fact that they are marginalized must not be a reason for treating them as sacred cows.

Indigenous resistance alternatives

In the first stage of the European invasion of Abia Yala – the first stage of an interminable war – our religions, our lands, our mines, our crops were laid waste, profaned and passed into the hands of those who had not worked them. Those of our fathers who had not been exterminated preferred to live 'as Christians', subject to the colonists' violence, valiantly resisting attacks, accepting Christian images. These were strategies of struggle, says Bruno Aymara, becuase the question was how to resist. Our forefathers accepted the images, the baptisms, the Christian sacraments, and used these things to clothe those elements of our cultures which were most important: Pachamama, Kukulcan, Yumbil, Paba . . .[13] Our fathers did not find reasons for their resistance in Christianity; they found them mainly in their own religions. The survival of the indigenous peoples with their religions is in spite of Christianity. Our fathers were confronted with an aggressive, anti-indigenous, self-imposing and dominant religion, except in areas where brave dissidents arose who questioned the system. For many years the church stuck to the idea of a single culture and defended Europe's monocentrism. And even today it does not always altogether free itself from this in its relations with our communities. The church has always been very sensitive to human rights, to the poor and needy, the marginalized in the dominant society, but when it has been a question of the 'other', she has regarded him as an enemy, a pagan, infidel, Moor, Indian. . . . in other words they are *different*. They are others who do not think like her, others who have their own visions of the cosmos, their own value systems. She has found it difficult to have any dialogue with these others, except when she has felt herself to be in the minority. But most of the time she has engaged in subjection, suppression, domination.

The Latin American bishops speak of an 'option for the poor' and place us in the category of poorest of the poor. But this option is not for the *other*; it is for those who are oppressed and trampled on in the dominant consumer society. Here we are reduced to a class. They cannot see the richness of what has been resisting for five centuries and our duty to contribute with our own special gifts to harmony among peoples.

Our indigenous communities have shown in various ways that they are offering very special alternatives of resistance in order to survive. Here we mention a few.

Cultural and religious revitalization

In the Kuna language this is called '*pabgan e nagkannar nudaked*' (dust, clean, polish, perfect, set out and make useful the legacy of our ancestors). Some call it 'cultural rescue'; others 'returning to the ancients', and some a 'search for identity'. In reality it is not just a cultural rescue so that the indigenous is not completely lost, nor a question of collecting indigenous documents for a future generation. It is a matter of returning in these moments of resistance and advance to the reason for survival, the reason for our fathers' strength. This will redouble our will to self-determination as peoples, convinced of our richness and our duty to make a special contribution to our brothers and sisters who suffer like us. This will bring about a more human world for all, in fellowship with nature, our mother earth. It is not a matter of confining ourselves to reserved places and events, living in the past with a phobia against developing society. That would be a naive way of looking at the need for self-determination in our indigenous peoples. None of our communities throughout Latin America accepts isolation. Either consciously or inspired by the media, our communities try to approach developing society. Now we must deepen our reasons for survival or death; that is, indigenous people must know what they sacrifice when they opt for the dominant society and what they gain in this interaction. They must become aware of their responsibility to contribute from their own particular richness in offering alternative ways of living for the whole of humanity. Only when our peoples realize what they possess and what they can lose, are they on the way to being really able to liberate themselves. In the words of one of our Kuna leaders, it is a matter of 'knowing why our grandfather's bow is dripping with blood, and what they did to him, why they killed him and why they reject us so much. But is it true that it is all over?'

Another of the signs of resistance we have been using throughout Abia Yala is that what I have described above very briefly leads us to demand laws guaranteeing our rights. It is logically absurd that the owner of the land should ask permission to live on his land.

Demand for land to be demarcated, return of stolen lands. Here the church must also take a decided stand in relation to indigenous lands in many regions of Latin America. At continental level many indigenous groups are in the process of formulating or reformulating laws deriving from our socio-political, religious and culture values . . .[14] We demand that national states should really accept socio-political structures that are multi-ethnic or multi-national and reject a false notion of a single national, Latin culture. We demand our own spaces, enabling us to offer new structures that can be alternatives for a society that is dying by swallowing its own tail.

Conclusion

We indigenous people do not live only by recalling the past. Our history is alive, and hurts us as it hurt our grandmothers and grandfathers. The history of the European invasion of our lands is a very long one and continues to massacre us. We are still in the middle of an unjust war.

The credibility of the church which carries the good news will be judged in accordance with its real and historical repentance. Clear pastoral directives for the indigenous are not sufficient. They must be translated into real action. We indigenous people see the church divded within herself into opposing sides. One part of the church is on our side, thinks of us as brothers and sisters and encourages us to go on advancing, resisting with new strength. It trusts in us and wants us to be authentic, it struggles together with us and also dies together with our people who fall. Another part of the church is aggressive; it squeals at the first blow from the indigenous, it tells us that we should be grateful to it for the gospel and for the lives of its missionaries. It thinks of us as children, says it is our mother and is always right. It guesses at what we want and never bothers to check; it sticks to its old structures and seems capable of sacrificing our lives to its ancient convictions and forms. The other sector of the church is the indifferent. These do not care whether we exist or not. Bishops, priests, nuns, laity may be ignorant of the indigenous people in their own countries. They say they are a waste of time; there are more serious problems in Latin America; the problem of the Indian is a false problem. It can be resolved with a few more schools to integrate them quickly and efficiently and without pain to anyone. This sector of the church does harm to our communities, it is an enemy in the war. But we have hope in the friendly part of the church . . .

Translated by Dinah Livingstone

Notes

1. Words of an Aymara Yatiri: meeting of Indigenous Peoples, La Paz, Bolivia, 24, 25, 26 November 1988.
2. Embera leader: programme of the Embera General Congress, El Salto, 1 February 1990.
3. Digna Rivera, Bribri: Aboriginal Pastoral Meeting, Palmar Sur, Costa Rica, 2, 3, 4 December 1989.
4. Saila Kuna Manuel Smith: meeting of Church Base Communities in Kuna, Panama, 6, 7, 8 November 1989.
5. Ngobe Sukia: Tole Meeting, Panama, 21, 22, 23, 24 August 1987.
6. Since before the arrival of the Europeans the Kunas have known this land as Abia Yala, meaning: ripe land, big mother land, land of blood. And today we have had imposed on it the name of the Italian (America).
7. Term used by the Panama Kunas to designate the category of non-indigenous, foreigner, white man.
8. Paez leader, Colombia: meeting of Indigenous Peoples in Bogota (church), 24, 25, 26 March 1988.
9. Taken from the conclusions of the indigenous meetings: Bogota 1988; Quito 1986; Palmar Sur 1989.
10. Puebla no. 34.
11. We studied this at our Aboriginal Pastoral Meeting (Palmar Sur, 1, 2, 3 December 1989), where we had the opportunity of meeting forty indigenous fellow pastoral workers (thirty ethnic groups and sixteen religious denominations).
12. Quechua leader: Aboriginal Pastoral Meeting, Palmar Sur, Costa Rica, 1, 2, 3 December 1989.
13. Mother Earth and names of supreme indigenous beings (Aymara, Quechua, Maya-quiché, Kuna).
14. Case of indigenous Kunas (1925, 1962, 1989): Aymara, Quechua, Maya-Quiché, indigenous Brazilians.

II · The Witness of Those who Suffer

1492: The Violence of God and the Future of Christianity

Pablo Richard

I. The violence of the conquest

There is no reason or excuse for being unaware of or forgetting the truth of the events which began in 1492 in what is now Latin America and the Caribbean. In 1492 death came to this continent: the deaths of human beings, the death of the environment, death of the spirit, of indigenous religion and culture. I want briefly to review here the basic details of the death of human life, which is the culmination of all deaths.

Modern studies calculate the indigenous population south of the Rio Grande (modern Latin America and the Caribbean) in 1492 at 100 million people.[1] It is thus terrifying that the estimate of the indigenous population in 1570 is no more than 10–12 million.[2] There can be no doubt that this is the greatest genocide in the history of humanity. Bear in mind that in that century Portugal had around one million inhabitants, and Spain and England about three million each. No European city, perhaps with the exception of Paris, was bigger than the capital of the Aztec empire, Tenochtitlán, which, when Cortés arrived in 1521, had 300,000 inhabitants. The Roman empire at its greatest extent was not greater than the Inca empire.[3] The indigenous population of Brazil in 1500 is put at five million; today, in a Brazil which has more than 140 million inhabitants, only 250 million indigenous survive.[4] According to CIMI (the Brazilian Catholic Church's agency for indigenous peoples), ten ethnic groups will disappear for ever in the next decade. In Mexico in 1532 there were around seventeen million indigenous; in 1608, just over one million were left, a genocide of sixteen million in seventy-five years.

In addition to the indigenous genocide, in Latin America we have the slavery of the blacks brought from Africa. This too was a long-drawn-out and far-reaching genocide. Three million black slaves were brought to Spanish America during the colonial period. For Brazil the figure to 1850 is four million.[5] To this we must add three million black slaves in the English and French Caribbean.[6] This gives a total of ten million black slaves in South America and the Caribbean, and these figures are conservative: other writers double this figure, and the number increases if we include the Africans who died on the voyage.

This genocide has many causes. First there were the extremely cruel wars of the conquest, in which massacres of whole indigenous communities were frequent. Another factor was the ill-treatment and the forced labour imposed on the conquered indigenous, the disintegration of families resulting from the forced labour of women. And there were the diseases. But another factor which had a direct influence on the genocide of the indigenous communities was the cultural and spiritual destruction of the people who inhabited this continent. The indigenous accounts of the conquest are impressive, with their subjective and collective interiorization of death. I will quote here only one of these texts, which admirably summarizes the indigenous vision of the conquest and the genocide and brings out the magnitude of the crime:

It was only because of the mad time, the mad priests, that sadness came among us, that Christianity came among us; for the great Christians came here with the true God; but that was the beginning of our distress,
the beginning of the tribute, the beginning of the alms, what made the hidden discord appear,
the beginning of the fighting with firearms,
the beginning of the outrages,
the beginning of being stripped of everything,
the beginning of slavery for debts,
the beginning of the debts bound to the shoulders,
the beginning of the constant quarrelling,
the beginning of the suffering.
It was the beginning of the work of the Spaniards and the priests,
the beginning of the manipulation of chiefs, schoolmasters and officials . . .
The poor people did not protest against what they felt a slavery,
the Antichrist on earth, tiger of the peoples,
wildcat of the peoples, sucking the Indian people dry.
But the day will come when the tears of their eyes
reach God and God's justice
comes down and strikes the world.[7]

This is the truth of the events, the truth of history about the genocide of the indigenous and Afro-Americans in America. Of course, there were also positive things during the conquest, and there were prophets who denounced the 'destruction of the Indies'. Many missionaries showed goodwill and generosity, and we can also recognize that, despite the conquest, there was some evangelization of America: the indigenous peoples were able to distinguish the liberating gospel of Jesus Christ from oppressive Western Christendom. But the whole of the positive side cannot wipe out the horror of the greatest genocide human history has known. We have to answer for this genocide, in radical solidarity with the victims, as theologians and as a church.

II. The violence of theology

The genocide and the massacre which began in 1492 would not have been possible without an appropriate theology. The historical violence was accompanied by theological violence. It is not possible here to go into the complex discussion of the theology of the sixteenth century,[8] and I wish to concentrate, as an illustration, on a single theologian of this century, Juan Ginés de Sepúlveda, and on one of his writings, *Tratado sobre las justas causas de la guerra contra los índios*.[9] Sepúlveda was born in Spain around 1490 and finished his treatise in 1545. Why do I choose this theologian? First, because he is usually ignored. Second, because he represents the antithesis of Bartolomé de las Casas. Third, because he is a tremendously lucid and universal theologian (he says clearly what everyone thinks and does), and, finally and most importantly, he is a theologian who uses theology to break with the biblical and theological tradition and to subordinate theology to the historical rationality of the conquest, which he calls 'natural law'. Sepúlveda's treatise was banned, not because it contradicted Fray Bartolomé de las Casas and the King, who at this point was keeping a certain distance from the conquistadores, but because Sepúlveda set out too clearly the rationale of the conquest and the war against the Indians, arguing for actions which ignored the imperatives of the gospel and faith. Sepúlveda, in offering a reasoned justification of what was happening in America, destroyed the very imperial ideology of 'evangelization' as a justification for the conquest. He used theology to prevent the production of a theological critique of domination. While his book may have been momentarily banned, his thinking is a faithful reflection of the reasoning behind the conquest and the genocide.

It would be impossible to summarize Sepúlveda's ideas here. I shall simply mention the theoretical elements of the *Tratado* which explain the sixteenth-century genocide. Sepúlveda discusses the conditions for a just war, first in general and then as applied to the American situation. The first three general causes are: the need to repel force with force, the need to recover things unjustly taken and to inflict due punishment on evildoers. But these conditions would seem to justify the Indians' war against the Spaniards. Accordingly Sepúlveda adds a fourth general condition, which he regards as less theological and more 'natural':

> Bringing to submission by force of arms, if this is not possible by any other means, those who by their natural condition should obey others but refuse their authority. The greatest philosophers declare that this war is just by law of nature (p. 81).

When Sepúlveda returns to the conditions for a just war and applies them to the American case, what was the last condition becomes the first:

> It is just and natural that prudent, honest and humane men should rule over those who are not so . . . [and therefore] the Spaniards rule with perfect right over these barbarians of the New World and the adjacent islands who in prudence, intellect, virtue and humanity are as much inferior to the Spaniards as *children* to *adults* and *women* to *men*, since there exists between them as great a difference as that between *wild and cruel races* and *races of the greatest clemency*, and between *the most intemperate* and the *continent* and *temperate*, and I would say between *apes* and *men* (p. 101, emphasis added).

The Spaniards' war against the Indians (whom Sepúlveda calls 'barbarians' and *hombrecillos*, 'midgets') is just, he says, because,

> though being by nature servile, the barbarians, uncultured and inhuman, refuse to accept the domination of those who are more prudent, powerful and perfect than themselves, a domination which would bring them very great benefits, and it is in addition right, by natural law, that *matter* should obey *form*, the *body* the *soul*, *appetite reason*, *brute beasts* human beings, *the wife her husband*, *children a father*, the *imperfect* the *perfect*, the *worse the better*, for the universal good of all things (p. 153, emphasis added).

In another place he adds:

> What more beneficial and salutary fate could have befallen these barbarians than to be under the rule of those whose prudence, virtue and religion will convert them from being barbarians who hardly deserve the name of human beings into civilized men, insofar as they are able to be such, from being slothful and libidinous into being honest and

honourable, from being irreligious and enslaved to demons into Christians and worshippers of the true God (p. 133)?

One is struck by the oppositions Sepúlveda constantly makes:

barbarians: Spaniards
children: adults
children: parents
women: men
apes: human beings.

The relationship of subordination is as essential and natural as that between:

matter and form
body and soul
appetite and reason.

If the body and the appetite rebel, the soul and the reason must exercise violence against them; in the same way, if the Indians rebel against the conquistadores, the conquistadores must exercise violence against them. Sepúlveda even justifies the torture of Indians, who 'thanks to terror combined with preaching have received the Christian religion'.

These texts, and these intrinsic relationships, are so clear that they need no commentary. What is extraordinary is the intrinsic correlation in Sepúlveda between colonial domination and racist, patriarchal and sexist domination. All these texts assert a logic of conquest and domination which totally escapes from theological and biblical reflection. Everything derives from necessity, obviousness and nature. Theology and faith are made subordinate to this natural and necessary logic, and Sepúlveda thereby succeeds in subordinating the church to the conquest and the logic of the gospel to the logic of oppression. And this was in fact what was happening. Faith was left on the fringe of the exercise of domination. Imperial ideology justified the conquest by evangelization. Sepúlveda justifies the conquest directly by an appeal to the logic of domination, presented as natural law, and subordinates the church and theology to this logic.

III. Current challenges for the church and theology

In the conquest and colonization of America, both through the violence of the events and through the violence of theology, Western colonial Christendom lost all its credibility, especially for its victims, the indigenous and black peoples of this continent. If Christendom continues to survive, it is not because it has credibility, but because it has power to impose itself. The future of Christianity and of the Catholic Church in Latin America and the Caribbean involves a radical critique of Christendom. This is what the theology of liberation is doing, and the result is the birth of the so-called church of the poor. This is a new *model* of church, opposed to the Christendom model. It is not a different church or a parallel church, but *a different way of being church.*[10] The church of the poor, or whatever it is called, is the model which is trying to replace Western colonial Christendom, whose actions and theology brought about the massacre of the Indians and Afro-Americans on our continent. The theology of liberation and the church of the poor came into being the instant there was political and theological questioning of the conquest and of Christendom, and this happened from 1492 onwards. The essential source of this critique has been the victims and those who took their part.

There are two elements which I believe to be essential to a critique of Christendom, elements which could enable Christianity and the church to recover their credibility after the abandonment of Christendom. One is *defending the lives of the indigenous peoples* and the other is the construction of a *liberating indigenous hermeneutic* by the indigenous themselves. There are many other elements, but I shall show that these two are essential and, moreover, give us a strategy for this period of the commemoration of the 500 years.

(a) Defending the lives of the indigenous peoples

Today in Latin America and the Caribbean there are about fifty million indigenous people.[11] That is 10% of the population, since our continent has about 500 million inhabitants. The countries with the largest indigenous populations are: Bolivia (71%), Guatemala (66%), Peru (47%) and Ecuador (43%). Then come Belize (19%), Honduras (15%), Mexico (14%) and Chile (10%). All these figures are conservative, since governments try to reduce significantly the statistics of indigenous peoples in their countries. Many people think that the number of indigenous peoples in Latin America and the Caribbean could be as high as eighty million.

Death faces the indigenous peoples today exactly as it has ever since 1492. Genocide continues in countries like Guatemala. Almost everywhere indigenous peoples are deprived of their land, or confined to 'indigenous reserves', where indigenous groups live as though on borrowed or mortgaged land, since they have no greater legal protection. Indigenous peoples are marginalized and discriminated against in education and health services, and in housing. Normally they are not allowed formal education in their own languages, and their cultural and religious traditions are not respected. Their nutritional and health standards are abysmal. They are exploited commercially and by foreign tourism. The natural environment where they live is destroyed, and the earth raped. Worst of all, they are continually humiliated, marginalized, discriminated against, banned, as peoples, races, ethnic groups and cultures. The dominant churches, for their part, continue to be European, Western and white; any sign of the growth of an Indian church is banned and checked. Indigenous liturgy is banned. Indigenous religion is relegated to the sidelines. Attempts to develop an indigenous theology of life are frustrated. There are very few indigenous bishops or priests.

If the church which was part of the system of colonial Christendom took part in and gave legitimacy to the conquest and the genocide of the indigenous peoples, this church can only regain its credibility by defending the lives of indigenous peoples. This is not just a matter of a work of mercy or compassion, or a purely preferential option. What is at stake in the survival of the indigenous peoples is the glory of God, the essence of the gospel, and the future of the church. After 500 years, whether the church lives or dies is bound up intrinsically with whether the indigenous peoples live or die. The church has irrevocably entered the history of the indigenous peoples. As Christendom it entered as a force for death; as the church it can only be a sign of life within their history if it saves the Indians' lives. Saving the Indians' lives means saving them as peoples, as ethnic groups, as races; it means saving their physical lives, saving their land, their labour, their health, their homes, their culture and religion, their environment, their participation, their identity, their spirituality, their freedom. At stake in all this is the life of the church and the credibility of God.

Recently the church has begun to do something. We should single out Bishop Leonidas Proaño, 'the Indians' bishop', who died on 31 August 1988. As bishop of Riobamba, Ecuador, he fought for an 'indigenous church'; he did much, but Christendom never listened to him. In Ecuador Bishops Alberto Luna and Gonzalo López have continued his fight. Many other bishops are committed to the cause of indigenous liberation: Pedro Casaldáliga in Brazil, Carlos María Ariz in Panama, Samuel Ruiz, Bartolomé Carrasco and José A. Llaguno in Mexico, and many others; many priests, religious and theologians (women as well as men) and lay people have also given their lives to the indigenous cause. They are still isolated and persecuted prophets, because the Latin American church, as a whole and as an institution, still does not accept responsibility for the genocide of indigenous peoples, does not take the part of the victims of the conquest, and does not make the defence of Indian lives the centre of its evangelizing mission.

(b) An indigenous biblical hermeneutic

When John-Paul II visited Peru he received an open letter from various indigenous movements which contained the following passage:

> John-Paul II, we, Andean and American Indians, have decided to take advantage of your visit to return to you your Bible, since in five centuries it has not given us love, peace or justice.
>
> Please take back your Bible and give it back to our oppressors, because they need its moral teachings more than we do. Ever since the arrival of Christopher Columbus a culture, a language, religion and values which belong to Europe have been imposed on Latin America by force.
>
> The Bible came to us as part of the imposed colonial transformation. It was the ideological weapon of this colonialist assault. The Spanish sword which attacked and murdered the bodies of Indians by day at night became the cross which attacked the Indian soul.

This text challenges us and pushes us towards conversion, but I think we should adopt a more radical and dialectical attitude, not to *give back* the Bible but to *make it our own*. The problem is not the Bible itself, but the way it has been interpreted. The indigenous peoples must construct a new hermeneutic to decolonize the interpretation of the Bible and take possession of it from an indigenous perspective. The Bible gives us testimony of the word of God, but it is also the canon or criterion of discernment of the Word of God today. It is important for the indigenous people of God to take possession of this canon in order to use the Bible as an instrument of prophetic discernment of Christianity and a radical critique of Christendom, so that the Bible and Christianity can regain the credibility which colonial Christendom destroyed.

An indigenous biblical hermeneutic must follow two basic principles. The first is to recognize the history, the cosmos, the lives and the cultures of the indigenous peoples as God's *first* book. The Bible is God's *second* book, given to us to help us to read the first. This idea is based on an ancient idea of St Augustine's, according to which God wrote two books, the book of life and the Bible. The Bible, God's second book, was written to help us to decipher the book of life. The Bible was written to give us back eyes of faith with which to look at the world, so that we could transform the whole of reality into a great revelation of God. The Bible is an instrument, a criterion, a canon, for discerning the presence and revelation of God in indigenous culture and religion.

The second principle is the recognition of the indigenous as the *authors* of biblical interpretation. Indigenous people must be able to appropriate the Bible and interpret it in terms of their own culture and religion. Of course this indigenous appropriation of the Bible must take place in the church, with its tradition and its magisterium, but the authors remain the indigenous people. These two principles summarized here are already being applied in the Latin American biblical movement associated with the Christian base communities, through the method we call a people's reading of the Bible.[12] This indigenous hermeneutic of liberation is growing up in the indigenous communities themselves. It is the indigenous people themselves, as the people of God, who are liberating us from oppressive colonialism and rebuilding a future of credibility and hope for the church.

Translated by Francis McDonagh

Notes

1. W. Borah and S. F. Cook, *The Aboriginal Population of Central Mexico on the Eve of the Spanish Conquest*, Berkeley, 1963: quoted by H. –J. Prien, *La historia del Cristianismo en América Latina*, Madrid 1985, pp. 77–8.
2. H. J. Prien, op. cit., p. 78.
3. Cf. 'Amerindia. Povos indígenas antes da chegada do branco', *Tempo e Presença*, Rio de Janeiro, No. 242 (June 1989).
4. B. Prezia and E. Hoornaert, *Esta terra tinha dono*, Sao Paulo, 1989, pp. 71–2.
5. H. –J. Prien, op. cit., p. 77.
6. E. Dussel, op. cit., p. 239.
7. Maya testimony from the prophecy of the book of the Linajes (Chilam Balam de Chumayel), quoted by M. L. Portilla, *El Reverso de la Conquista*, p. 86.
8. On this see the excellent book by F. Mires, *En nombre de la cruz. Discussiones teológicas y políticas frente al holocausto de los índios (periodo de conquista)*, San José 1986.
9. Mexico, Fondo de Cultura Económica, 1979 (Bilingual edition, Latin–Spanish).
10. This is the main thesis of my books *Death of Christendoms, Birth of the Church* (New York 1987) and *La Fuerza espiritual de la Iglesia de los Pobres* (San José 1989).
11. Cf. 'Amerindia. Povos indígenas antes da chegada do branco', *Tempo e Presença* (Rio de Janeiro), No. 242 (June 1989).
12. Cf. *Revista de Interpretación Bíblica Lationamericana* (RIBLA), San José, Costa Rica, No. 1 (1988). This issue is a monograph entitled *Lectura Popular de la Bíblia en América Latina. Una Hermenéutica de la Liberación*.

Conquered and Violated Women

Julia Esquivel

The conquistadores

All men. In the fullness of their physical force and driven by a great ambition, gold and glory. Some petty nobles; the majority poor, with no name of note in Spain and no possibility of winning one at home.

Almost all with some military rank, owners of weapons more powerful than those of the warriors of this continent. Two important factors in their superiority were horses and gunpowder. The psychological effect of both was perhaps similar to that produced by bombers on unarmed peasant populations in some counter-insurgency wars today. These two weapons turned them into creators of terror. They used them as sources of strength, strategic deception and even myth.

They regarded the task of subduing, subjugating and enslaving as a favour to the inhabitants of the New World. This certainty drove them to make the continent Spanish and seal this achievement with religion. Severo Martínez says:

> This means that the armed struggle was only a means, a device for achieving economic subjugation, and that this last aim was the decisive element in the conquest. And it can also be shown that evangelization was a third phase, the ideological subjugation necessary, like the military phase, for the consolidation of the economic conquest.

When the *conquistadores* reached here, they thought that they had reached the riches and products of the Orient, and this belief blinded them. Many of them did not realize when they arrived that they were looking at *the other face of the world*.

As a result, when they arrived, they invented the 'Indians', although the peoples of these lands already had names. When they realized their mistake they did not correct it. In creating the Indians they reinforced the ever-growing advantages of their domination over them. Severo Martínez says again:

> This means that when the social group of the creoles began to develop and defend the prejudice of their Hispanic superiority – a basic prejudice in the ideology of the group – the determining factor in their effective superiority over the Indians was not Spanish descent in terms of flesh and blood, but the inheritance of the conquest in terms of wealth and political power. Enjoying very favourable conditions of life, they were able to farm and develop all the capacities which had not been able to develop among the Indians.

The imposed identity of 'Indians' and its whole burden of submission, dependence and servitude grew during the consolidation of the conquest, the so-called colonization. With it grew the power and wealth of the invaders and their descendants, and conversely the underdevelopment of the 'Indians'. Frantz Fanon gets it exactly right when he says that 'Colonialism cannot be understood without the possibility of torturing, raping and killing.' They had no limits.

The women

In order to get an idea of the significance of the treatment of Indian women during the conquest and colonization we need to spend a little time to understand how European women were treated in this period. When the Spaniards arrived, there were differences between one people and another; it was not a homogeneous world. Women were not treated exactly alike in all societies. Although some of them enjoyed a certain freedom, and even a degree of social authority, the great majority lived under male tutelage, in patriarchal and authoritarian societies. They were prepared to be conquered. They were familiar with submission to the male as a condition for survival. Conquest and domination by the Spaniards increased their defencelessness, because, like the land and the gold, they became the property of the victors. Their bodies became land to be conquered because they had been the property of the men who waged the war. All wars, and especially wars of conquest, bring with them the violation of women. By virtue of this fact men think and feel that they become stronger by invading and possessing women's bodies. The act of taking the women of defeated men affirms them in this sense of power.

The defeat, the capture or flight of the men places the women in a situation of vulnerability and defencelessness such that opposition on their part to the will of the victor can bring more prolonged sufferings, not just for them, but also for their children. The woman thus feels obliged by these circumstances to remain silent and submit to save her life and those of her children. If she remains subject to just one man, or the first passes her on in turn to different men, her situation is so complex that in order to stay alive she almost has to deaden her senses. Many had children by one or several Spaniards.

The accounts of the Spanish chroniclers talk much more about the booty, the war itself, Christianization, and relatively little of the Indian women. The little they do say has to do with physical abuse of the women as objects of sexual pleasure and also as servants or slaves.

'Official' concubinage was given the name *barraganería*, and in order to be admitted to it the woman had to be baptized first. Indian patriarchal tradition allowed and encouraged Indian men to give daughters of nobles to the Spaniards to seal an alliance, as occurred in Europe, and they also offered women temporarily as a sign of hospitality, as they offered food or gifts.

The women were almost always abandoned when their owner married a Spanish woman. Cortez married some of his captains to women he had raped. Examples are the daughters of Moctezuma, and Malintzin, a slave used as a 'tongue', that is, Cortez' translator and interpreter. She came to be indispensable to him since she spoke three languages. She was exceptionally beautiful. This woman's life shows very well that even the women who lived with Spanish men for relatively long periods were never treated as equals, any more than the Spanish women. Like the 'Indies', the Indian women were taken, invaded, used and their individuality and culture were ignored.

Malinnalli Tenepal was known as Malintzin or Malinche, the origin of the word *malinchismo*, to be a traitor, a collaborator with the enemy, the one in power. Malinnalli was the daughter of the chief Xaltipan. She was stolen in time of war by Ollinteutli, chief of Olutla, who offered her to the captain Juan de Grijalva, who commanded the Catholic king's fleet which sailed from Cuba to Yucatán in 1518. The girl was thirteen years old and of cheerful disposition. She was brought richly dressed, accompanied by Ollinteutli's high chiefs and maidens singing wedding songs.

No sooner on the boat than she was baptized by the priest Juan Díaz. That same night, when the boat started back for Cuba, she was raped by Grijalva. When they reached Cuba, Grijalva rejoined his wife and gave the girl to Alonso de Hernández Portocarrero, who was related to the nobility. Malintzin lived with her new owner for some time, and learned Spanish, as well as speaking Náhautl and Maya. The expeditions which came and went from Cuba, and her knowledge of Spanish, enabled her to begin to understand in her own way the spirit and ways of these Christians. Later Portocarrero took her with him to Cozumel and other parts of the continent. She saw battles and massacres, always as the property of Portocarrero and subject to the plans and decisions of men.

As a result of the differences between the *conquistadores* and the accusations against Cortez, Cortez sent Portocarrero to Spain as procurator to defend him against the charges made against him. Portocarrero was imprisoned in Spain and Cortez took over Malintzin for his sexual caprices and to use her as a 'tongue'. Noticing that the captains and officers were coming up to talk to her, Cortez isolated her completely, ordering that no one should talk to her and appointing Juan de Arteaga to keep watch on her day and night, even when she attended to the needs of nature. These events gradually changed the cheerful character of the young woman. She lived like this the whole time. Cortez made her pregnant and, when he discovered, married her to Juan Jaramillo on the expedition to the Hibueras when Jaramillo was unconscious as a result of a drinking bout. When he came round, he objected to 'such a great lord transferring his obligations to him', but nevertheless profited from the situation. Though Cortez had ordered her to be married, Malintzin had to stay at his side all the time, during all the expeditions and battles, to be his 'tongue'. She was always watched by Arteaga.

When the conquest of Mexico was largely secure, Cortez was obliged to leave for Spain to defend himself against innumerable charges and demands before Charles V, and, with Jaramillo's agreement, stole Malintzin's little son from her. The boy was born on the unsuccessful expedition to the Hibueras in a very difficult situation for Malintzin. She brought him up on her own until the age of four, until he was taken from the house in which she lived with Jaramillo. Malintzin also had a daughter with Jaramillo. When this daughter was two, five days before the trial of Cortez before the Residency was due to begin, at which Malintzin had been told she would be called as a witness, Malintzin was murdered in her house with thirteen knife-blows at dawn on 24 January 1529. Jaramillo robbed Malintzin's daughter of all her mother's property when he married the Spaniard Beatriz de Andrade.

It was very common for Indian women of high rank, daughters of kings and chiefs, to be taken and used sexually by the *conquistadores*. They were then given to officers and later to common soldiers. They were treated as objects and nullified as human beings.

According to the researcher Otilia Meza, from whose book I obtained these details:

And Hernando Cortez, to whom she had been an excellent 'tongue' as well as concubine, never recognized her valuable help, which had brought him so much glory, and his ingratitude reached such a pitch that he shamefully forged her name on the famous lying 'Cartas de Relación' which he wrote to Charles V, informing him that 'an Indian woman' had married Xuan Xaramillo and given him as a dowry the villages of Olutla and Tetiquipaje in the province of Coatzacoalco. He then gave Malinalli the village of Kolotepec, in Mexico the mansions of Jesús María and Medinas, the gardens of Moctezuma in Chapultepec and a plot of land in San Cosme.

For the sake of these lands, and for the prestige of being Cortez' 'friend', Captain Jaramillo did the *conquistador*'s bidding, and was probably an accomplice in, if not responsible for, Malintzin's death.

This story is just one example among many.
      And they took them, picked out the most beautiful, those with light brown complexions. Some women, when they were taken, smeared themselves with mud and wrapped an old, torn cloak around their hips and put a rag as a shirt over their busts; they dressed in old rags. And on all sides the Christians probed. They opened their skirts, rubbed their hands all over them, over their ears, their breasts, their hair (Sahagún).

And [Cuauhtemoc's] martyrdom began. He bore it with dignity, in silence. His young wife, Tecuichpo – Cotton Tuft – daughter of Moctezuma, suffered the fate reserved for women prisoners of war. Cortez raped her and gave her to his soldiers, then took her back again and later made her pregnant (Héctor Pérez Martínez, *Cuauhtemoc*).

And some chiefs . . . did not waste time. They did not abandon their wives and children, but went to great lengths to place them in safe-keeping near the houses, on the other canal . . . And then too the women fought in Tlatelolco, throwing lances. They dealt blows at the invaders; they were dressed as warriors (*Visión de los vencidos*, Anonymous chroniclers of Tlatelolco).

The admiral gave me a most beautiful Caribbean woman, and as she stood their naked, as is their custom, I felt a desire to go with her. I tried to carry out my desires, but she would not consent, and attacked me in such a way with her nails that I wished I had never started. But when I saw this I took a rope and beat her, and she screamed. Finally we reached such a state of agreement that I can tell you she was brought up in a school of whores (Letter of Michele de Cunco, 1492, quoted in Todorov, *La Conquête d'Amérique*).

The powers established in the course of these 500 years, and the armies and police forces – sometimes trained by so-called developed countries – use methods no different from those used by the *conquistadores*. The Indian peoples in the interior of our countries still live in states of defencelessness and vulnerability which makes them easy victims of abuses of power.

> The ferocity in the massacres and the cannibalism goes with an unrestrained sexual violence and a machismo which makes the woman into an animal to give the soldier pleasure, and afterwards, when she's no more use, she can be murdered. Sometimes we've seen the soldiers queue up to rape a girl, and afterwards she was like a rag. And our brothers who survived the massacre and have gone back to the macabre scene of the events found our women naked or with their skirts up (*Guatemala: Government against the people*).

> When they rape a girl or a woman, they line up and go one after another. Then, when they've all had their turn at raping the poor woman, they kill her (Indigenous from the war zone of Huehuetenango).

> And we too have realized that the army has taught the soldiers to be arrogant and take liberties with women, and rape them, even in peace-time. We've found this in the capital: they practise on our sisters who work as domestics in their houses. The violence is accompanied by this arrogance, although sometimes they use deceit or flattery to get their way (Tribunal Permanente de los Pueblos, Sesión de Guatemala: Genocidio en Guatemala).

> *Answer*: After it was all over, then . . . and they shut the door on us in the court, and after they shut the door, since the window has one, two, three small holes, we were looking. Well, they went in and took our wives out of the church. They took twenty, some took ten. They went in groups among the houses, and then they started ra- , they started raping the women there in the houses. They finished raping them, and then they shot the women and then, after they'd killed them they set fire to the houses.
> *Question*: So they raped them and afterwards killed them by shooting?
> *Answer*: Yes, and finally they set fire to the houses and the houses all burned down. They went in among, among the houses and went in groups of fifteen or ten, the soldiers went with the women. They'd go in groups of ten or maybe fifteen, twelve soldiers. First they raped them, then they killed them . . .
> *Question*: In groups they . . .

Answer: In groups, yes, in groups. They went with the, with our wives. And then all our children, like the women . . . were shut in the church . . . and they were crying, our poor children, they were screaming, they were calling us, but in the end they died. (Masacre de San Francisco: la muerte de las mujeres, Huehuetenango, Guatemala, 17 July 1982).

Abuses committed by police and soldiers were daily events in Guatemala in the 1980s.

The challenge

Jewish exegesis offers us a very important way of reading the story of the creation of human beings as male and female. The reading suggested is: 'he took one of the sides' instead of 'one of the ribs'.

> If Adam is alone, it is not because the man-woman couple does not exist, but because the couple is in a situation in which the future pairs do not know each other and are unable to dialogue.
>
> This myth of the Hermaphrodite is both a biological and a psychological reality. We have already said that every human being is the seat of a double polarity: they are at the same time male and female, in their genes and in their psychological make-up . . . In the ancient world and in the middle ages the woman used to be shown behind the man. Only the man could really see the future; the woman's view was blocked – all she saw was the man.
>
> Yes, exactly, alongside. It's true that for many centuries in most civilizations the place of the woman was behind the man, rather than alongside.
>
> The midrash, I think, takes us beyond that. It teaches us that God did not want to create the woman behind the man, or alongside him. He wanted something deeper for human beings, a face-to-face sexuality. The woman should be in front of the man, facing him, 'shining face to shining face' . . .
>
> God placed the woman in front of Adam, facing him, because she is his future (Abecassis and Eisenberg).

In the Song of Songs there is a developing process of this experience of meeting which leads to this 'face to face'. The expressions the two use, man and woman, are a journey of discovery full of a marvellous reciprocity. Throughout the poem there is a series of searches, absences, meetings, which again and again keep giving rise to the experience of wonder in the presence of the other person who is completely equal and yet different.

This wonder reminds us of Adam's first reaction to Eve, 'This is bone of my bones and flesh of my flesh!' Before Eve appeared in front of him Adam had been unable to find real companionship. He had had enough time to see, reflect and realize that it wasn't in human nature to behave like the animals. Among them the male is controlled by the rhythm of the female's coming into heat. Both basically respond to a biological programming.

The man, in contrast, suffers an absence; he is alone. It is something bigger, more than biological necessity. He yearns for a companion to fill this emptiness. His complete fulfilment depends on his being able to love and be loved. His desire cannot attain full satisfaction; for the sexual relationship to be human, it must be a relation of love.

The rabbis interpreted the creation of Eve in terms of the separation of the two halves of the Hermaphrodite, with the clear intention of comparing them to the two sides of the Tabernacle or the Temple. Both were the site of the presence of God. In this way they were saying that God is present in the union of man and woman.

Instinctive possession, merely to satisfy a bodily need, expels God from the relationship, that is, drives out the possibility of loving, of fullness. It also produces divorce as the death of the relationship. Reducing the woman to an instrument of animal satisfaction was what the *conquistadores* did, and there were no controls on it. The same spirit is encouraged today by the consumer society.

Neither the discovery nor the conquest have ended in Latin America. It has not been possible to have an authentic discovery because of the conquest and the spirit of the conquest alive today in the policies of the great powers. Our true human and cultural identity has been constantly distorted since the coming of the *conquistadores*. We have passed from one servitude to another, exposed to pressures and interventions by economic, political and military powers trying to dominate us. Under these conditions women have been invaded, colonized and raped, if not in their bodies, then in their personalities and their identities, as so many testimonies of Indian women bear witness. The Indian peoples have had to adopt an attitude of submission in order to survive, and adopt a form of resistance which disguised their true nature. Very often this resistance took the form of revolt, always in unfavourable conditions, such as flight to the remotest parts of the jungles and mountains to save their lives and preserve a minimal space of freedom until today.

The plea of Esther, the young Jewess chosen to satisfy the desires of King Ahasuerus, expresses this attitude of submission in order to save one's life while waiting for a favourable moment to secure freedom. In her outburst she lets her true identity escape:

You have knowledge of all things,
and you know that I hate honours from the godless,
that I loathe the bed of the uncircumcised,
of any foreigner whatever.
You know I am under constraint,
that I loathe the symbol of my high position
bound round my brow when I appear at court (Esther 4.17u).

Like Esther, our peoples are prisoners of an identity and a destiny imposed by the powerful of the earth. Those who decide our destiny, from within or without, sometimes do not know our geography or our languages, far less our aspirations for life and freedom.

We women and peoples of Latin America have so far been only beginning to understand how vital it is for us to understand who we are and where we are coming from if we are to be able to choose what to believe and how to live. As long as 'the stronger' does not attain a truly human balance which enables him to recognize us as bone of his bone and flesh of his flesh, there will not be true humanity. Man-woman will be the image and likeness of God when we obtain this equality in difference, flourishing in a creative, fruitful harmony, in the couple and in the relationships of all peoples and societies. The clay of our beings as persons and peoples, moulding itself freely in genuine encounter, in mutual discovery and reciprocal respect, will make possible the impossible.

The prophet drowns our hope with light:

On every lofty mountain, on every high hill
there will be streams and water-courses, on the day of the
great slaughter
when the strongholds fall.
Then moonlight will be as bright as sunlight
and sunlight itself be seven times brighter
– like the light of seven days in one –
on the day Yahweh dresses his people's wound
and heals the scars of the blows they have received (Isaiah
30.25–26).

In the Maya cosmogony as in so many others, the sun corresponds to the male and the moon to the female. The prophecy says that the instant we achieve equal brightness, the brightness will be perfect; the people's wounds and scars will be healed. With this healing will come what is now impossible: irrigation channels and streams will water the highlands, and they will be able to become farmland, these *altiplanos*, now semi-barren, to which the Indian peoples of America were pushed out. Equality of access to true development will make both the male aspect and the female aspect shine, and will enrich both, without detriment to either. This maturing will mark the *kairos* for the rising again of true life on the earth as the home of all.

Translated by Francis McDonagh

Books cited

Severo Martínez Peláez, *La Patria del Criollo*, Costa Rica 1985

Otilia Meza, *Malinalli Tenepal, la Gran Calumniada*, Mexico 1988

Historia General de las Cosas de la Nueva España, Mexico 1989

G. Baudot and Tzvetan Todorov, *Relatos Axtecas de la Conquista*, Consejo Nacional para la Cultura y las Artes, Mexico 1990

Ricardo Falla SJ, *Masacre de la Finca San Francisco, Huehuetenango, Guatemala, 17 julio 1982*, Copenhagen 1983. Tribunal Permanente de los Pueblos, *Sesión sobre Guatemala, Madrid, enero de 1983: Genocidio en Guatemala*

Ricardo Falla SJ, Centro de Investigación y Acción Social de Centroamérica (CIASCA)

Josy Eisenberg and Armand Abecassis, *Et Dieu' créa Eve. A Bible Ouverte II: Présences du Judaïsme*, Paris 1979

Bernal Díaz del Castillo, *Historia de la Conquista de la Nueva España*, Mexico 1964

Josefina Oliva de Coll, *La Resistencia Indígena ante la Conquista*, Mexico 1988

Jacquies Lafaye, *Los Conquistadores*, Mexico 1988

Humiliated and Exploited Natives

José Oscar Beozzo

We are the conquerors of death.
Our race will not die out as long as there is light in the morning star.
Popol Vuh (sacred book of the Maya)

Introduction

Who are the so-called 'natives' of America? Today they are around seventy million people, present in all the countries of Latin America except Uruguay and the Caribbean countries. In Guatemala and Bolivia they make up the majority of the population, while in Ecuador, Peru and Mexico they are the base of the rural population and of the migrants on the edges of the big cities. In other countries, such as Brazil, Chile, Argentina, El Salvador and Costa Rica, they have been reduced to hard-pressed minorities. They are the heirs of an ancient history, one which goes back, according to recent discoveries, 42,000 years, with its roots in the continents of Asia and the islands of Polynesia. When the Europeans arrived in Latin America, the 'natives' formed an extremely rich mosaic of peoples, speaking more than 2000 languages, of which a quarter survive to today. Some were grouped in small clans of forty to fifty families, while others were organized in vast empires, such as that of the Aztecs, with around twenty million subjects, or the Inca empire, with a slightly smaller population but extending for over 5000 kilometres, from the south of Colombia to the River Maule in Chile, an area greater than that of the Roman empire at its height. For comparison, Spain at the time of the conquest had a population of 3.5 million people, and Portugal one million. These peoples lived by hunting, fishing and gathering fruits, and in addition by domesticating plants and animals by which they developed into great agricultural civilizations. Alongside the rice of Asia, the wheat which spread along the Mediterranean basin, the native peoples of Latin America created civilizations based on maize (Mexico, Central and South

America), cassava (the Caribbean and South America), the potato (the Andean plateau), and in addition gave us some of the basic plants and fruits of today's world: cocoa, tobacco, quinine, rubber, pepper and peppers, the avocado and the pineapple.

Of these peoples, some have a background of centuries of contact, from the time of the conquest, while others continue to shun it. In Brazilian Amazonia some twenty remote groups continue in isolation and without contact with the white world. Confronted with the quincentenary (1492–1992), leaders of fifteen different indigenous nations, meeting at an ecumenical consultation at Quito in Ecuador, declared their total repudiation of triumphalist celebrations for the following reasons:

1. There was no such discovery or genuine evangelization as has been claimed, but an invasion with the following consequences:

(a) Genocide through the war of occupation, infection with European diseases, death from excessive exploitation and the separation of parents from children, causing the extermination of over seventy-five million of our brothers and sisters.

(b) Violent usurpation of our territories.

(c) The fragmentation of our socio-political and cultural organizations.

(d) Ideological and religious subjection, to the detriment of the internal logic of our religious beliefs (*II Consulta Ecuménica de Pastoral Indígena – Aporte de los pueblos indígenas de América Latina a la teologia cristiana*, Quito 1986, p. 85).

This, then, is the context within which we shall tackle the subject of humiliated and exploited natives, attempting to bring together the threads of the past and the present, and mentioning the movements fighting to regain the lost dignity. 'Humiliation' refers directly to anything which offends the dignity of the human person and the cultural, moral and spiritual values of a community or people. 'Exploitation', on the other hand, more closely implies the economic realm and the politico-social and legal mechanisms used to legitimate various forms of forced, or at least unpaid, labour. Exploitation always comes accompanied with some sort of humiliation, and attains perfect symbiosis when slavery is brought in to improve the exploitation. Stripped of any right, the person is now reduced to the legal status of a chattel, like a beast of burden, and is listed in commercial contracts like any other commodity, as illustrated in the Spanish Philippine code of the sixteenth century.

I. Offended and humiliated

Humiliation is something global and indivisible, but it can come about in different ways. The process of conquest and colonization removed from the indigenous peoples the status of masters of their own destiny, forcing them to bow to the commands and whims of another. The image of the bowed Indian, the physical expression of his new fate, in contrast with his previous erect posture, is already to be found in this Mayan verse from the first half of the sixteenth century: 'Straight and tall were their bodies then,' (Chilam Balam de Chumayel, in M. L. Portilla, *A Conquista de América Latina vista pelos índios*, Petropolis 1984, p. 60; M. L. Portilla, *El reverso de la conquista*, Mexico [13]1986).

A. *Political humiliation*

The irreparable trauma of the conquest, with its train of destruction, was also engraved on the memory of the indigenous, as shown by this sad song, probably composed in 1523, immediately after Cortés' capture of Tenochtitlan, the capital of the Mexica:

> Mourning spreads.
> Tears drop there in Tlatelolco.
> The Mexicans have already sailed off,
> looking like women;
> the flight is general.
> Where are we going, friends? So it was true?
> They have already abandoned the city of Mexico . . .
> Weep, my friends.
> Know that this means
> we have lost the Mexican nation (ibid., p. 48).

In the Inca empire the massacre of Cajamarca, the arrest of Atahualpa and his murder after a mockery of a trial, completely disorientated the people, as can be seen from this elegy for Atahualpa:

> Under foreign rule, martyrdoms piled up, destroyed,
> confused, led astray, refused memory,
> alone;
> dead the protecting shade,
> we weep,
> without anyone to turn to.
> We are losing our minds (Portilla, op. cit., p. 100).

B. *The humiliation of women*

Another text, by the anonymous author of Tlatelolco, written in 1528, also touches on the humiliation inflicted on the indigenous women:

. . . And when they were taken prisoner, the population began to leave, looking for somewhere to settle. When they left, they were in rags, the poor women with the flesh of their buttocks almost bare. And on all sides the Christians examined them. They parted their clothing, everywhere, stroked them, their ears, their breasts, their hair (ibid., p. 44).

This was merely the beginning of a process which placed on one side white men, Europeans, militarily, politically and ideologically victors, and on the other women from a defeated people. The famous Latin American interracial unions never take place between an indigenous man and a European woman, but between a European man and an indigenous or African woman, as a member of a defeated people and almost always a servant or slave, rarely as a wife. Guaman Poma de Ayala, the Quechua who wrote the harshest indictment against the abuses of the colonial system, made a pathetic appeal to the king to remove from the indigenous settlements Spaniards, blacks and mulattos, the cause of an interracial mixing which was gradually destroying the indigenous world, because the product of these unions was always an addition to the world of the colonizer and the end of not just the cultural, but also the very biological reproduction of the native peoples:

. . . And he saw yet another province of Indian women turned into whores, each burdened with half a dozen *mestizos*, mulattos, every sort of mixture. Being such great whores, they no longer want to marry their equals, the Indians . . . And so the said Indians disappear, and do not multiply, and the settlements become depopulated and die out (Felipe Guaman Poma de Ayala, *Nueva Coronica y buen gobierno*, Mexico 1980, III, p. 119).

c. Humiliation of the survivors condemned to die

This same experience of implacable and gratuitous destruction, of a death foretold and inflicted, of a threat to the ethnic, cultural and spiritual survival, is today the lot of the Yanomami people on the border between Brazil and Venezuela. They have lived in the area for 3000 years and were one of the last untouched cultures of America. Now they are being destroyed by the neglect of the Brazilian government, which closed its eyes to the invasion of 40,000 goldminers who are poisoning water-courses with mercury, raping women and children and transmitting venereal diseases, influenza, malaria and tuberculosis, all deadly to the Yanomami. The plea of spokesman Davi Yanomami, who recently received the United Nations Global 500 award, is a perfect echo of the laments of the sixteenth-century poets:

The government is not respecting us. It thinks of us as animals . . .

I am a Yanomami. We Yanomami thought that the white man was good for us. Now I am seeing that it is the final invasion of indigenous land; the others have already been invaded.

They came to take our land. They are taking it.

The same thing happened out there with other Indian brothers in America. Now it is happening here in our land.

The government should not do this. It knows that we are the oldest Brazilians, that we were born here, we are called Yanomami . . .

All they know about is dealing in money.

Our thinking is land.

Our interest is to preserve the land, in order not to create diseases for the people of Brazil, not just the Indians . . .

We Yanomami are dying because of diseases: malaria, influenza, dysentery, venereal diseases, measles, chickenpox and other diseases which the Indians didn't know, brought by the goldminers from outside.

We can't cure these diseases, our shamans can't . . .

Our way is better than that of the whites because we preserve the rivers, streams, lakes, mountains, the game, the fish, the fruit – cabbage-palm, bacaba palm, the nuts, cocoa, cocoawood, wine-palm, what already exists, what Oman created.

I, Davi Kopenawa Yanomami, want to preserve all this . . .

We Yanomami want the mountains to be preserved, we don't want them to be destroyed. We want these places to be preserved so that our history, our spirits, are not brought to an end.

We would like the whites to understand this ancient history and to respect it (Davi Kopenawa Yanomami, 'Declaration to all the Peoples of the Earth', Boa Vista, Roraima, 28 August 1989, duplicated).

What links the sad poems of the peoples defeated at the conquest and Davi Yanomami's desperate plea in the face of the genocide of his people is the same final result: a people turned into strangers in their own land, stripped of their territory, of their history, of their memory, devastated by disease and death, the survivors treated like animals.

D. *Humiliation in the world of symbols*

But there is a humiliation which is deeper and more subtle because it adds to the material destruction a symbolic destruction which deprives a whole people of reasons for living and surviving. Language and religion are the basic structure of this dimension, and were to be used as a deliberate instrument of domination. An example for language is the evidence of the

Marquês de Pombal, the all-powerful executor of the enlightenment policies of José I of Portugal (1750–1777). Pombal forbade the use of indigenous languages in Maranhão and Brazil (then separate territories), even in catechesis, and explained the theoretical basis for the ban in his 1757 Directory for the indigenous villages of the Amazon region:

> It has always been a Principle unswervingly followed in all Nations which conquered new Dominions, immediately to introduce among the conquered Peoples their own Language, because it is indisputable that this is one of the most effective Means to remove from rustic Peoples the barbarity of their ancient Customs; and Experience has shown that in the same Degree that there is introduced the Language of that Prince, which has conquered them, there is rooted in them Devotion, Veneration and Obedience to the said Prince (*Directorio que se deve observar nas povoações dos Indios do Pará, Maranhão*, Lisbon 1758, no. 6, in: J. O. Beozzo, *Leis e Regimentos de Missão*, São Paulo 1983).

From the north of the continent to the south, the indigenous languages banned by the colonial state remain banned by the national states, with the exception of Paraguay, where Guarani is recognized as a national language alongside Spanish, although in practice the whole of public life takes place in Spanish, with Guarani relegated to the status of a domestic language. The indigenous person's mother-tongue becomes a weapon of discrimination, humiliation and scorn. Hear the testimony of this Guatemalan Indian, pressed into the army: 'From the first day I arrived at the barracks I was told my parents were mad' – and he too – for being an Indian. 'My parents are mad because they can't talk properly, and I was to be taught to speak as people ought to speak. So they began to teach me Spanish, and gave me a pair of shoes, which I found painful to wear. But I had to wear them or I was beaten. They beat me until I got used to them' (E. Burgos, *Yo me llamo Rigoberta Menchú*, Mexico 1968, p. 174).

Conversely, recovering one's language is a source of human and spiritual rebirth. When the Aymara indigenous communities of Lake Titicaca succeeded in forming themselves into the Aymara Methodist Church, they started the process which led to their having a liturgy in Aymara and Aymara ministers and bishops, in a clear affirmation of their rediscovered dignity and identity.

Dom Pedro Casaldáliga, bishop of Sao Félix do Araguaia, has written a preface to a grammar of the language of the Tapirapé, a tiny people once on the verse of extinction but now reviving. He comments:

> Writing a people's grammar may be simply codifying a past, but it can also be giving more systematic support to a future. The written language

is like the infrastructure of the spoken soul. The authors of this grammar . . . are banking on the future of the Tapirapé nation. They want to assist in the affirmation of a people in danger of extinction thirty years ago, but now increasing in offspring, in ethnic awareness and in active campaigning to secure their own lands and self-determination.

The Tapirapé Indians, original authors and owners of their language, written or spoken, will discover themselves in this grammar, as in a family album, and will affirm themselves with it as Tapirapé by speaking Tapirapé. They have already saved their land, though it has been moved and reduced time after time. May they also save their language in full. May they survive, grow and flourish as the Tapirapé people (Ameida et al., *A lingua Tapirapé*, Rio de Janeiro 1983, pp. 1–2).

If language is the symbolic field which structures everyday life and thought, religion provides reasons for living. In America we find it too turned into a deliberate weapon of domination, through the intimate connection between the state's political and economic aims and the church's missionary goals, amalgamated in the institution of royal patronage, in both Spanish and Portuguese territories. The evidence of Barleus, a Dutch Calvinist and chronicler of the period of the Dutch occupation of the Brazilian North-East (1630–1654), shows how this use of religion is common to colonial schemes: 'To strengthen our power, we certainly make use of religious opinions. Each takes whichever religion he has chosen as a suitable instrument for seeking security, for the furtherance not only of human salvation, but also of domination' (G. Barleus, *História dos feitos recentemente praticados durante oito anos no Brasil*, São Paulo, Itatiaia, Belo Horizonte 1974, p. 71). This twofold interaction of political domination and religious imposition is what leaves the indigenous world no escape from its situation of defeat, not just military but also spiritual. It is the despairing cry which rings out from the dramatic dialogue between the first twelve Franciscans in Mexico (1524) and some of the learned Aztec priests, survivors of their nation's tragedy. The Aztecs said:

> You said that we do not know the Lord who is near and with us, he who owns the heavens and the earth.
>
> You said that our gods were not real. This talk of yours is new, and it disturbs us, it makes us uneasy . . .
>
> We are simple people, we are perishable, we are mortal. Well, let us die, let us perish, since our gods are already dead' (Portilla, op. cit., pp. 20–21).

II. Exploited and enslaved

The indigenous peoples of America were very soon to understand the implacable logic of the conquest, its motivation by an insatiable greed for gold. The accumulation of wealth in the hands of the Europeans could not be accomplished without a systematic plundering of the material possessions of the American indigenous and without their exploitation as labour in the colonial economy.

A. *Tribute and violence*
The Mayan texts on the conquest already contain an awareness of the burden of poverty which was to follow the conquest:

Alas for you,
my younger brothers.
In the Seventh Ahau Katun
you will have a surfeit of pain
and a surfeit of poverty
from the tribute collected
by violence
and above all paid swiftly!
You will give a different tribute the next day
and the day after.
This is what is to come, my children.
Prepare to bear this burden of poverty
which is coming upon your peoples (Portilla, op. cit., p. 62).

B. *Gold and greed: plunder of goods and slave labour*
Guamán Poma, the Peruvian Indian, already old and bent, spent thirty years combing the highways and byways of Peru in search of 'the poor of Jesus Christ' – his name for the indigenous people impoverished by colonial exploitation. He has left eloquent descriptions of the greed of the Spaniards: 'Day after day they did nothing but think about gold and silver and the wealth of the Peruvian Indies. They were like a desperate man, mad, insane, all sense gone through thinking of gold and silver' (Poma de Ayala, op. cit., p. 347). They satisfied their greed by subjecting the indigenous peoples to servitude, exploiting them without limit: 'And they sought relief by doing great evils and harm to the Indians, asking them for gold and silver, taking their clothes and food. The Indians were terrified at seeing people the like of whom they had never seen before, and so throughout the kingdom they hid and fled from the Christians' (Poma de Ayala, op. cit., vol. II, p. 347).

This exploitation, which began in the Caribbean islands, later spread to the so-called *terra firma*, taking the classical forms of the *encomienda*, Indians handed over with their land to a large landowner, or the *mita*, Indians removed from their villages to work in the mines, and the *obrajes*, Indians, but especially women, forced into sewing, weaving and producing ceramic articles for the colonial society. These forms of forced labour have left us the prophetic condemnations of a Montesinos, in his Advent sermon of 1511 on the island of Hispaniola:

> Say with what right and justice you keep these Indians in such cruel and horrible slavery. By what authority have you waged such detestable wars on these peoples, who were living on their own lands, inoffenssively and peacefully, and exterminated such vast numbers of them, with deaths and slaughter the like of which was never known? How can you keep them so oppressed and weary, without giving them food or relieving them in their sicknesses, from which, because of the excessive labours you force on them, they fall sick and die or, better, you kill them, so that you can seize and acquire gold every day? (Bartolomé de Las Casas, *Historia de las Indias*, Mexico, 1986, vol. II, book III, p. 441).[1]

We also have the passionate and systematic denunciation by Las Casas of the endless exploitation to which the American Indians were subjected. Far from being exaggerated, the evidence offered by Las Casas of the 'destruction of the Indies' is increasingly regarded as consistent with the continuing findings of research in historical demography.

c. Indigenous or African slavery?

Las Casas' naive hope that the importation of African slaves might alleviate the exploitation and suffering of the indigenous peoples, and his failure to see that all forms of slavery are equal, and that there cannot be a distinction between American and African natives, led him to make a humble confession of his error:

> Before the [sugar] mills were installed, some of the residents who had some assets which they had acquired with the sweat of the Indians, and their blood, desired to obtain permission to buy some black slaves in Castile, since they could see that their Indians were dying out. There were even some who promised the cleric Bartolomé de las Casas that if he brought them, or obtained permission for them to bring, a dozen negroes, they would allow the Indians they possessed to be set free. Hearing this, the said cleric, who, since the King had come to the throne, enjoyed great favour, as was seen above, and the remedies for these lands had been placed in his hands, obtained the King's consent

that, in order to free the Indians, the Spaniards of these islands should be allowed to bring some black slaves from Castile (J. B. Lassegue, *La Larga Marcha de las Casas*, Textos, Lima 1974, p. 139).

Las Casas soon saw that exploitation of blacks came on top of exploitation of the Indians and did not lessen it:

> Not long afterwards the cleric repented of the advice he had given, judging himself guilty by inadvertence, because, as he subsequently saw and confirmed . . . , the captivity of the negroes was as unjust as that of the Indians. Nor was his advice that negroes should be brought so that the Indians could be freed an effective remedy, even though he presumed that they [the Indians] were captives for just cause. However, he was not convinced that his ignorance and goodwill in this matter would excuse him before the divine judgment. At that time there were on this island ten to twelve negroes . . . , but when the first permission had been given and expired, many others were granted continually, with the result that more than 30,000 negroes were brought to this island, and over 100,000 to these Indies as a whole, to the best of my belief, and for all that the fate of the Indians did not improve, nor were they freed . . . (ibid., p. 140).

D. Exploitation and theology

In this exploitation of American Indians and black Africans, one aspect which interests us is the involvement of theological reflection, which on the one hand stood up to cry for justice and on the other became entangled in the justifications and legitimation of the system of slave labour as an acceptable means of evangelizing Indians and Africans. Was there an awareness that what was at stake in this issue was not just the credibility of the gospel, but the very concept of God, a God of life, defender of the poor and humble, or a God allied with the powerful in their authoritarianism and exploitation? Montesinos does not hesitate to threaten the Spaniards: 'You may be sure that in your present state you cannot be saved any more than the Moors and Turks who lack faith in Jesus Christ and do not even want it' (ibid., p. 78).

Guamán Poma, for his part, concludes that because of their greed for gold and the ill-treatment they inflicted on the Indians, all the Spaniards will go to hell: magistrates, priests, landowners (Poma de Ayala, op. cit., Vol. II, p. 347).

Many indigenous leaders were able to see through the colonial system and unmask the real theology which sustained and gave meaning to the adventure of the conquest and colonization: 'The god of the Spaniards is gold' (cf. Gustavo Gutiérrez, *Dios o el oro en las Indias – siglo XVI*, Lima

1989, especially Chapter III: 'Gold, mediator of the gospel', pp. 107–33). What is at issue now, as we approach the quincentenary of these events, is the humiliation and exploitation inflicted, then and now, on indigenous people and Africans supported not only by a political aim but also by a theological vision. The direction the indigenous peoples are taking today, and the Latin American black movements, are both asking for a theology which breaks with the idolatry contained in the colonial enterprise. There was the idolatry of greed, the idolatry of gold, which infected both lay people and clerics, state and church, but there was also a more subtle idolatry, that of the European, Western, version of Christianity, set up as a kind of untouchable idol to which all the indigenous cultures were sacrificed after being dismissed as demonic. The culture was labelled demonic to give grounds for destroying it. That is why it is still so difficult for the indigenous face of God to emerge in Latin America, and yet without it the recovery of the dignity of the indigenous peoples and the preservation of their origins will remain incomplete. As well as economic and social liberation, the indigenous peoples of Latin America are longing for a cultural and spiritual liberation. The condemnation of the exclusivism of the Western version of Christianity is present in this beautiful and tragic Mayan poem, which uses the symbolism of the flower, so central to the culture:

> Then everything was good
> and then the gods were cut down . . .
> Wasn't that what the foreigners did
> when they came here?
> They taught us fear,
> came to make the flowers wither.
> To let their flower live
> they damaged and swallowed up our flower . . . (Portillo, op. cit., p. 60).

Conclusion

The glory of God is that all flowers should survive and that the indigenous cultures should be able to flourish once more, uttering the name of God in their many languages and praising him in the particular genius of their customs, dances and songs.

Any commemoration of the 500 years must include, as an essential element, a penitential gesture, translated into effective reparation on the part of the various states and of the church. The states have the responsibility for guaranteeing or restoring indigenous lands, which have always been stolen or under threat, but without which there can be no indigenous life. They should also recognize the rights of indigenous peoples to their languages and customs, in a constitutional framework which defines Latin American societies as multi-ethnic and multi-linguistic.

The responsibility of the churches is to renounce the exclusivism of the Latin Western version of Christianity, the Anglo-Saxon Western, in the case of the Protestant churches, being prepared to accept the religious otherness of indigenous and Afro-American cultures. Internally they must work towards a respectful inculturation in the lives of indigenous and Afro-American peoples, embarking on an intransigent defence of their scorned rights, the day-to-day struggle for justice and for the end of racism, and adopting, joyfully, their spiritual world, so full of sorrows and wisdom, with centuries of commitment to life and imbued with resistance and hope.

Translated by Francis McDonagh

Notes

1. There is an abridged translation of Las Casas' History: Bartolomé de las Casas, *History of the Indies*, translated by André Collard, New York, Evanston and London 1971.

The Slave Trade and Black Slavery in America

Laënnec Hurbon

Slavery in the New World: a running cost of modern civilization

From Greco-Roman antiquity to the European Middle Ages, slavery did not change its nature in the regions of Asia or Africa and in the New World. Often perceived as an archaic form of exploitation (or even over-exploitation) of human beings by human beings, the phenomenon has proved susceptible to trivialization when it is measured only by its effects (the social degradation of the individual, racism, economic profitability, and so on . . .). But slavery raises a basic question about law and the history of freedom. Philosophy and theology have certainly had intuitions, but most of the time they have simply kept slavery as a metaphor for the domination of human beings by human beings, when they do not evacuate its specific content.

However, the history of the slave trade and the slavery of the Blacks which began with the discovery of the New World is still part of our modern world and of Western civilization, and is even the background without which neither anti-black racism nor the present under-development of the African continent would be comprehensible. There is a great temptation, which originates in the very nature of slavery – where it is practised – to dilute the event in universal history and thus to excuse the modern Western world a confrontation with what in fact is part of its own memory. Perhaps it is because Europe failed to consider the specific nature and the novelty of slavery in the Americas that it was so little prepared to recognize the possibility – inscribed at the very heart of its development – that it would produce other catastrophes like Auschwitz or the Gulags. In fact from the sixteenth century onwards, in slavery we see the relaunching of a system which, while remaining in continuity with the Middle Ages, extends over three continents, over a long period (four centuries), and sees itself aimed solely at economic profitability. Far from being a mishap for modern civilization or a simple historical accident, slavery in America bears witness to the foundation of this civilization and is even part of its running costs.[1]

Within the limits of this short article, I plan to recall the basic facts of the Black slave trade and its consequences for the whole of the Black Continent; then the practice of slavery in the three Americas with its organization and its justification; and finally the struggles of the slaves which led to emancipation. However, the most important thing is not to engage ourselves in the task of the historian, but to try to begin with the memory of slavery still fresh, and to go on raising questions of the most burning relevance about law and universality, asking whether slavery has not always been the institution which outlaws part of humanity at the very time when reason and the Enlightenment in the West are decking themselves out in fine array.

From Indian slavery to the Black slave trade

At the beginning of the sixteenth century, theologians, jurists and canon lawyers argued violently over the right of Spain to reduce the Indians to slavery. However, the practice of slavery was already well advanced. In 1495, 500 Indians were captured and sent as slaves to Spain. On 2 August 1530, it was all very well for Charles V to proclaim the illegality of Indian slavery, as a result of the stubborn and tenacious defence of the rights of the Indians put up by de Las Casas, but it was all up for the Indians. The *encomienda* as a system of forced labour used to develop the gold mines meant certain genocide for the newly-conquered people. The Indians were also thought to be unsuitable for slavery. But there was never any debate, whether legal or theological, over the Blacks of Africa. We know that. The myth of the son of Ham, who was under a curse, was in circulation at the end of the Middle Ages, and this authorized first Portugal, and then Spain, to draw slaves freely from the 'Black Continent'. In 1434 the Portuguese bought cargoes of slaves from the North Africans in Africa for domestic work and agriculture generally, and for the sugar cane plantations on the island of Sao Thomé. And in the New World, while there was tearing of hair over the barbarism or the idolatry of the Indians, in 1503 'negro' slaves were working alongside the Indians and were now ready to fill the gap when the Indians disappeared. It was all very well for Las Casas, having indicated the suitability of the Blacks for slavery, to regret having been an accomplice in the slave trade, but by then the damage had been done. The powerful interests of the crown and the church presided over a practice of conquest in the face of which the very question of legality slowly disappeared.

Through '*l'asiento*' (the monopoly granted by the crown to a company to trade in Black slaves), Portugal was in the vanguard of the slave trade throughout the sixteenth century. But Spain disputed Portugal's possession of the new lands of the New World and appealed to the pope to arbitrate. So it was that in 1517 4000 slaves were sold and deported to Hispaniola and Cuba. In the footsteps of Spain, Holland, France and England vied with one another to take part in the trade. Chartered companies were created in a headlong rush. In 1635 the Compagnie des Indes de l'Amérique was instructed by Richelieu to provide slaves for the Caribbean islands. In 1651 England in turn founded the Guinea Company, and later, in 1672, the Company of Royal Adventurers; in the eighteenth century the country ended up by dominating the triangular trade through Liverpool, the greatest port for shipping negroes in Europe.

But how did people get slaves? First of all by establishing forts and bases all along the African coasts. At that time Africa, called the Gold Coast, the Slave Coast, the Pepper Coast, the Ivory Coast, was simply an immense depot of ebony and slaves, who were captured on the raids carried out in the interior or through the wars encouraged between the tribes by the slavers. Local potentates reinforced their power and sold prisoners of war and subjects whom they considered to be delinquent. Any means of responding to the European demand for slaves was legitimate. In exchange the Europeans brought fabrics, copper, glass and above all finery and firearms for the African kings. Little by little real negro states were founded and consolidated: Dahomey, Congo, Ashanti South Africa. Guinea, from where the slaves often came, is the region along the coast between the river Senegal and Sierra Leone, extending further to the Gold Coast and the kingdom of Angola.

The consequences of the slave trade were catastrophic for the African continent, if only because of the great hole which it made in the population. It is now reckoned that over four centuries, around 11,700,000 slaves were deported to the three Americas; some writers talk of thirteen, even fifteen, million.[2] At all events, we have to add those who died during the wars of captivity and during the crossing. According to C. Coquery-Vidrovitch, the average mortality rate was 13%.[3] During the eighteenth century, England alone provided between two and three million slaves for its colonies, for those of France and Spain, and for Virginia. In the same period France transported around one million slaves on 3321 ships. In 1774, black slaves in the southern United States numbered 500,000. And it is reckoned that around two million slaves were at work in Brazil in 1798. There was not a single English, French, Spanish, Dutch or Danish colony which was not provided with slaves. In 1788 Jamaica was the most prosperous of the English colonies with 256,000 slaves, while St Dominique was the greatest source of wealth for France with 405,828. These impressive figures indicate that the African continent must have undergone a real cataclysm at a demographic level. The young (male and female) were captured in the largest numbers. Slaves over forty were usually rejected by the traders, though their demand for negroes was never completely satisfied. So Africa must have undergone an acceleration in its decline. Craftsmanship, weaving, metalwork, agriculture, dropped into second place in the face of a trade which led to the domination of a slave system in the majority of states, with the result that at the very moment when Europe finally agreed to give up slavery, at the end of the nineteenth century, by a strange irony of history Africa seemed devastatingly crippled, since by then one in four Africans were slaves.[4]

We must pay particular attention to the calvary of the Atlantic crossing. It took around forty days, in ships in which sometimes between 400 and 500 slaves were chained two by two at the feet and stacked up in the holds (like lines of books). Hunger, diseases like scurvy, dysentery and so-called 'putrid fever' made the slave ships floating tombs. Even in the eighteenth century, on a single ship (the *Iris*) 131 slaves died out of 966; there are other examples of 110 out of 442 or even 193 out of 401. And what about ill-treatment? That is the wrong way to put the question, since by definition the slave, a piece of livestock, was open to any excess on the part of his or her proprietor. That is the first thing to be noted about the everyday life of the slave.

The institution of slavery

As the negation of the protection of law and of rights to a human being, the slavery of the New World was an institution the justification for which was provided by positive laws laid down by the modern state that arose in the sixteenth and seventeenth centuries. What were the motives for this institution? What objectives and what interests did it serve? What contradictions does it reveal in the modern Western world, but also in Christianity, which, as we shall see, would prove to be a keystone in the ideological justification of slavery? We can only really explore these questions if we pay careful attention to the specific conditions of the everyday life of the slave on the ground in the New World.

An abundant literature has already taken stock of these conditions, and here I need only sum up their essential features. The slave was a slave for life, and any children were destined to slavery. That already indicates the degree to which slavery was the very empire of death. However, this was a slow death, even if the life-span of the slave – virtually throughout the Americas – was estimated at seven years. Work under the supervision of a taskmaster was from sunrise to sunset and was enforced by the discipline of the whip – about which it is necessary to be more specific: between 50 and 200 strokes were the penalty for the least negligence. To be a slave was to be a beaten body which in this state had to make its full contribution. Any interpretation of the attitude of the masters in paternalistic terms is deprived of its foundation here. For the master had to work rigorously – for the degradation of the slaves, for their complete and utter downfall, so as better to reduce them to what was considered to be their natural condition. In charge of feeding, clothing and housing the slaves, the master contrived to carry out these duties under a regime of pure favour and yet could not avoid parsimony. In 1666 Fr Dutertre tells us that adult slaves had a few rags for clothing, while the children were completely naked. The condition of the slave had to be made visible right up to death. Full of commiseration, the same Fr Dutertre, slaver though he was, reports that 'of fifty who die one buries only two in a shroud; people bring them covered with their own filthy rags or wrapped in a few canna leaves'.[5]

The tortures reserved for the rebellious or lazy slave are not evidence of the particular cruelty of some masters, but are part of the structure of the daily practice of slavery. To apply a red-hot iron to the tender parts of the slave, to tie him to stakes so that insects gnawed him to death, to burn him alive, to chain him, to set dogs or snakes at his heels, to rape negresses, and many such tortures, served above all to express absolute domination. And it was absolute, or rather it claimed to be: in the act of branding slaves, changing their names, mixing the races, making them lose all kinship, in short producing among them a cultural amnesia from which they emerged zombies, living dead totally subjected to the caprices and humours of their masters. But – and this is not at all paradoxical – the modern state did its utmost to relieve the master of the burden of having to think about this absolute domination for himself and assume responsibility for it.[6] The scandal of slavery was in fact dissolved, or at least defused by reasons of state and mercantile interests. How could one take account of the situation other than by questioning the legal and ideological system set up around slavery?

From the beginning, as we have seen, the slave trade presupposes a general accord within the European nations between the church, the state, the nobility and public opinion. Certainly the slave was already seen as a slave or a prisoner whose death penalty had been commuted into a social and legal death. From this perspective, slavery no longer provoked any questioning. Still practised in Europe in the twelfth and thirteenth centuries, and later in the fifteenth century, it had an arsenal of justifications to back it up. But as a result of the new experience of the slave trade in the New World, the modern European states put to the test not only their expansionist capacities but also their internal efficacy as an authority which could subordinate religion to itself and give it the pedagogical task of producing human beings.

Numerous disciplinary regulations, decrees, ordinances came from the great cities; they demonstrate their sustained interest in the survival of the institution of slavery. But among the legal frameworks that one can find in all the slave colonies of the New World, the French Black Code, the *Code Noir* of 1685, deserves special attention. Since it is impossible to give a detailed analysis of the text here, I must content myself with stressing that the objective of this code was not to relax the living conditions of the slave nor to contribute to limiting the power of the master, but to establish the order of slavery and reinforce it through the apparatus of the state. Republished in France in a new edition edited by Louis Sala-Molins, who describes it as 'the most monstrous legal text produced in modern times',[7] the *Code Noir* was seldom mentioned by the philosophers of the Enlightenment; it even fell into oblivion, though for two centuries it gave French slavery its essential structure.

What the *Code Noir* states is paradoxically that the slave has no rights and the master alone has any. None of the articles which describe the slave as a chattel, property, and thus as a 'thing' (in the sense that Roman law gives to the term) is embarrassed by the contradiction of submitting the slave to the royal tenderness and piety of the master who is to feed him, clothe him, support him, provide for his religious instruction, dispose of his offspring and avoid 'barbarous and inhumane treatment' (art. 26). But where the *Code Noir* pretends to protect the slave, at the same time it declares that the slave cannot in any instance bear witness or complain in person before the courts against the excesses of the master (art. 30). So on the one hand the slave is a thing or animal, and on the other a human being, but deprived (legally) of all rights. This situation is not at all, however, that defined by Roman law; it passes over that law from the precise perspective of the service which the modern state claims to be offering graciously to a whole continent, and to what is already being called a 'race'.

The objective of the institution of slavery is in fact to convert to Christianity infidels or pagans living under the empire of Satan. 'All the slaves in our islands shall be baptized and instructed in the Catholic religion . . .' (art. 2). Christianity does not develop the activity and defend the body of the slave; it serves the state by proclaiming to the slave his state duty, which is obedience to his master. Already slaves and captives on their continent, but also idolaters, the Blacks can only give thanks to providence for their deportation to America. 'Their servitude,' writes Fr Dutertre in the seventeenth century, 'is the principle of their happiness, and their disgrace is the cause of their salvation.'[8] This was to be echoed a century later, in 1776, by a disciplinary rule: 'Public security, the interest of the masters, the salvation of their soul, are the motives which must prompt the missionary to work at it (the religious instruction of the negroes) with all the greater zeal.'9 Conversely, meetings of slaves who attempt to go back to their African religious system are forbidden. They are regarded as occasions of rebellion. The maintenance of the ideological cover of slavery, i.e. forced conversion, also seems to have been an obsession with the administrators. Generally speaking, the clergy performed their role well enough; in fact they themselves owned slaves.10 Granted, some priests who protected runaway slaves or were too zealous in their instruction were rapidly deported and put on ships home.

As far as the state was concerned, the most important thing remained its complete hold over the life of the slave. Christianity, dedicated to barring possibilities of revolt among the slaves, had at the same time to perform a civilizing work, to serve as a place of access to Western culture, the parameters of which claimed to define humanity. However, for slavery to be maintained, the necessary logic was that slaves were unsuited to Christianity, that they were sorcerers and barbarians and basically flawed. How? By the inscription of these 'blemishes' on their biological constitution. If social prejudice was not the principle of slavery, it came to take its place and develop at the heart of the practice of slave-owning. The 'negroes' were suitable for slavery because they were a degraded species. To the myth of Ham was gradually grafted on an anthropology of the 'negro': savage and barbarous, cannibalistic, lazy, polygamous, prone to human sacrifices and with no taste whatsoever for freedom. A vast literature circulated in the eighteenth and nineteenth centuries,11 disseminating in Europe such an image of the Black as to render Western public opinion insensitive to the hell of slavery. To tell the truth, it was a hell given for a time of purgatory to the 'negro' who, for having forcibly been put in touch with 'civilization' (Western civilization), would one day deserve the quality of a human being – provided that that day was as far off as possible.

From slave resistance to abolition

Slavery in the New World was a tightly-knit system. To make itself that, it had to recapture the experience of ancient and mediaeval slavery and develop it to the full. The slaves had two primary ways out of it. Either they could leave their bodies to their masters and rejoin Africa symbolically or spiritually: suicide, abortion, the refusal of care or food, and infanticide, are the first expressions of a great rejection. Or, as an alternative, they could flee individually or collectively ('marooning').12 The cause of flight has often been sought in hunger or ill-treatment; in fact to run away was a gesture affirming freedom. Wherever possible, slaves tried to escape the power of their masters. Real slave republics were formed in Brazil, in Jamaica and in Guiana. And without any doubt, from the seventeenth century onwards, every regulation coming from the administrations or the capitals was aimed at the systematic repression of marooning. Some articles in the *Code Noir* are simply lists of a panoply of punishments to be imposed on the runaway slave.

Rumours of poisoning, revolts accompanied by burning of the plantations and sugar factories, haunted the sleep of the masters throughout the eighteenth century, especially in the islands. Soon, in the wake of the events of the French Revolution, St Dominique, France's most popular colony, with more than 400,000 slaves, offered the spectacle of the first major successful slave revolt. An insurrection sparked off during the night of 15 August 1791 was the inauguration of a long struggle lasting thirteen years, in the course of which the political genius of Toussaint Louverture emerged.

From the depths of their dereliction, the slaves were able to find within themselves the resources to express their dignity. Little by little they undertook the underground construction of a new culture in which they could recognize themselves. Thus for example Voodoo in Haiti, Santeria in Cuba and Candomble in Brazil, trance-cults inherited from Africa, form a regional creation with rich mythologies in which one can see a reinterpretation of lost Africa, and also of missionary Christianity. And the blues and negro spirituals still bear witness to a will to life and hope at the heart of imprisonment in slavery. Perhaps, too, the Black Americans have written a new page in the history of Christianity, by having been able to make the churches places of struggle for the recognition of their human rights.[13]

However, the march towards the abolition of slavery was one of extreme slowness. The abolitionist ideals expressed cautiously in the eighteenth century by the Enlightenment and supported boldly in England by William Pitt, Wilberforce and then by Clarkson, met with no success. Almost everywhere in Europe, the most radical philanthropic writings leant solely towards the suppression of the slave trade and proposed a gradual emancipation. In Paris in 1788 the Société des Amis des Noirs was from the start interested in the civic inequality between mulattos and whites in the French colonies, but not at all in an immediate abolition of slavery. News of the bloody revolution of slaves which broke out in 1791 had to reach Paris for people at last to become aware of the horror represented by Black slavery. But here again, the general freedom proclaimed on St Dominique in 1793 was not ratified by the Convention until 1794, and was then put in question again by Napoleon Bonaparte in 1802. The exceptional case of the new independent state of Haiti served as a foil to any immediate abolition, since it was said that abolition brought with it the risk of the loss of the colonies. While England succeeded in declaring the slave trade illegal in 1807, under the pressure of its Parliament and Protestant petitions, France followed, reluctantly, only at the Congress of Vienna in 1815. From this date until 1845, no less than twenty Franco-English treaties were signed before the achievement of the official cessation of traffic in slaves and abolition in France (1848). But illicit trading continued strongly with the southern states of the United States, with Brazil and Cuba, until 1870–1880. In fact Cuba was the last colony to proclaim abolition, in 1880.

The vicissitudes of abolition show the degree to which the slave trade and slavery were bound up with the economic interests of the great powers and what can well be called reasons of state. The vigorous polemic launched by Clarkson and the English Protestants, particularly the Quakers, and then by Abbé Gregoire and Victor Schoelcher in France against the anti-abolitionists, in fact came up not only against widespread prejudice against the Blacks in public opinion but above all against the European concern for expansionism. Abolition was only achieved at the point when it was possible to keep the prosperity of the colonists intact, and the riches brought to Europe by the slave colonies.

Certainly, with the theories of natural law developed in the seventeenth century, with Enlightenment philosophies like those of Kant or Rousseau, and with the Declaration of the Rights of Man in 1789, slavery was shown to be a scandal and a crime against humanity. But if we are to understand its long duration, two factors need to be taken into consideration: the tendency to sacralize the state through reasons of state, which has the virtue of undermining the universality of the principles of equality and freedom; and the tendency to make Europe the judge of all the other cultures, as a result of which a racist ideology with pretensions to being scientific underwent a spectacular rise, especially in the nineteenth century.

Are not the freed Blacks, having become poor peasants, workers, unemployed living in the shanty towns, household servants or migrant workers, still victims of racism? Yet again, the quest for equality and freedom is the order of the day, and remains the task which will open the horizon on which the humanity of humankind can appear. To achieve this, should we not detect in the movements of rebellion set off by slaves both a practical implementation of inalienable human rights and also the indication of a dream which has yet to be fulfilled, a dream which, in the midst of the many varied contemporary struggles for freedom, should be regarded as the duty of humankind?

Translated by John Bowden

Notes

1. For the novelty of the slave system in the New World see e.g. D. B. Davis, *The Problem of Slavery in Western Culture*, Ithaca, NY 1966; id., *The Problem of Slavery in the Age of Revolution, 1770–1823*, Ithaca, NY 1976; E. Genovese, *Roll, Jordan, Roll: The World the Slaves Made*, New York 1972; and the excellent collection edited by S. Mintz, *Esclave – facteur de production. L'économie politique de l'esclavage*, Paris 1981. But for the universal aspects of slavery see above all M. I. Finley, *Ancient Slavery and Modern Ideology*, London 1980; O. Patterson, *Slavery and Social Death. A Comparative Study*, Cambridge, Mass. 1982; C. Meillassoux, *Anthropologie de l'esclavage*, Paris 1986; or the very topical H. Vallon, *Histoire de l'esclavage dans l'Antiquité* (1879), reissued Paris 1988.

2. For the demographic facts of the slave trade see recent works like Serge Daget (ed.), *De la traite à l'esclavage. Actes du Colloque internationale sur la Traite des Noirs* (two volumes), Paris 1988; L. Crete, *La Traite des nègres sous l'Ancien régime*, Paris 1989; and the classic work by P. D. Curtin, *The Atlantic Slave: A Census*, Madison, Wisconsin 1969, which is now getting rather dated. For the importance of the slave trade in the industrial development of England see E. Williams, *Capitalism and Slavery*, London 1964; finally, for the figures put forward in the nineteenth century, before abolition, see Alex Moreau de Jonnes, *Recherches statistiques sur l'esclavage colonial et sur les moyens de le supprimer*, Paris 1842.

3. C. C. Vidrovitch, 'Traite négrière et démographie. Les effects de la traite atlantique. Un essai de bilan des acquis actuels de la recherche', in *De la Traite à l'esclavage* (n. 2), 57–70.

4. Ibid., 68.

5. J. B. Dutertre, *Histoire générale des Antilles habitées par les Français*, Paris 1666, II, 538–9.

6. See the argument which I have developed in the following articles: 'État et religion au XVIIᵉ siècle face à l'esclavage au Monde', *Peuple méditerranéens* 27–28, 1984, 39–56; 'Esclavage moderne et État de droit', *Chemins critiques. Revue haitiano-caraibéenne*, Port-au-Prince and Montreal, I 2, August 1989, 37–57.

7. L. Sala-Molins, *Le Code Noir ou le Calvaire de Canaan*, Paris 1986, 9; cf. also the critical analysis formerly proposed by L. Peyraud, *L'esclavage aux Antilles françaises avant 1789*, Paris 1897, and above all the rigorous work of A. Gisler, *L'esclavage aux Antilles françaises, XVII–XIXᵉ siècles*, Fribourg CH 1964, new revised and corrected edition, Paris 1981.

8. Dutertre, *Histoire générale* (n. 5), II, 502.

9. Quoted by Gisler, *Esclavage* (n. 7), 185.

10. Ibid., 193ff. In this work Gisler shows beyond even the established fact that clergy owned slaves, that the church sought more to alleviate the lot of slaves (though with rather feeble results) than to contest the institution itself.

11. For the image of the Black in France in particular see the exhaustive study by W. B. Cohen, *Français et Africains, Les Noirs dans le regard des Blancs, 1530–1880* Paris 1980; see also L. F. Hoffman, *Le Nègre romantique*, Paris 1972; in his article 'L'origine due racisme en Europe. Quelques hypotheses', *De La Traite à l'esclavage* (above, n. 2), 535–47, P. H. Boulle argues that racist talk develops with the appearance of the abolitionist movement.

12. For a general view of the importance of marooning, see R. S. Price, *Maroon Society*, New York 1973.

13. See the excellent discussion by E. D. Genovese, *Roll, Jordan, Roll: The World the Slaves Made* (above, n. 1), above all 168.

The Voices of Those who Spoke Up for the Victims

Maximiliano Salinas

The cry of the prophets in the New World: 'A voice crying in the desert'!

One of the voices raised simultaneously with the colonial invasion of the so-called New World, but at odds with it, was the cry of those who spoke on behalf of the victims. It was a prophetic criticism and protest from those who succoured the victims of the invasion, to free them or protect them from its violence. This word recreated the voice in the desert which announced the liberation of the exiles in Babylon (Isa. 40.3), itself taken up by John the Baptist to proclaim the possibility of conversion to the Kingdom (Matt. 3.3).

Fray Antonio de Montesinos, one of the greatest prophets of the New World, began his 1511 sermon with the words of the book of the Consolation of Israel and of John the Baptist: 'a voice of one that cries in the desert' (Matt. 3.3).

These voices, spread throughout America in the sixteenth and seventeenth centuries, had a force which even today inspires enthusiasm and shock, and form an essential discourse for us Latin American Christians. They are part of our own Bible. With the power of the Spirit they point to the magnitude of colonial oppression and the way to an encounter with the living God among the oppressed.

The colonial victim formed the context of the proclamation of the gospel of Jesus Christ, for conversion to the good news of the Kingdom of God for the benefit of these victims. The cry of the prophets was both a historical and a theological event. They knew from the Bible that the voices of the victims would rise up to God. Fray Luis López de Solís, bishop of Quito in 1597, wrote: 'The cries of these natives, because of the many and great hardships they experience at the hands of the Spaniards, reach the ears of

God.'¹ And like John the Baptist they were unswerving in proclaiming the messianic justice of this God. Fray Diego de Humanzoro, bishop of Santiago de Chile in 1666, wrote to the Holy See:

> The cries of the Indians are so great and insistent that they reach the heavens. And unless we go to the aid of these wretches or our ardent desire dries up their tears, I shall be called before the court of the same most just Judge . . . And those who oppress and insult the poor to increase their wealth will be condemned by the Lord.²

Where did the prophets of the New World come from? The prophetic movement which grew up after the conquest grew out of communities which brought together lay people, priests, religious and bishops to defend particular oppressed groups; one such was the Caribbean Dominican community in the sixteenth century which produced Bartolomé de Las Casas (1484–1566).

These people came from the invading European world, but were transported, by the power of the Spirit, to testify to the oppression of the victims and take their place. From that moment the New World became an unhappy land, laden with violence and therefore needing prophets. Juan del Valle, bishop of Popayán, said in 1551 that he felt he was living in the land of Babylon rather than the realm of the king of Spain. Fray Julián Garcés, bishop of Tlaxcala between 1528 and 1542, used Nineveh, the ancient cruel capital of the Assyrian empire, as a symbol of his episcopal see, adopting the role of the prophet Jonah ('Go to Nineveh, the great city, and proclaim to them that their wickedness has forced itself upon me' [Jonah 1.2]).

Fray Diego de Humanzoro understood his message as that of the prophet Ezekiel, the sentinel of his people, announcing God's judgment from the deportation to Babylon.

The Spirit enabled these Europeans to break out of the mind-set of the invaders. In particular, the Spirit led them to abandon the invaders' formal religion. This was the basis of Las Casas' experience in Cuba at Pentecost 1514, when he realized that an offering made to God without the practice of justice was stained with the blood of the poor (Ecclus. 34.18–22).

Becoming poor, adopting the place and the outlook of the poor, this was the programme of the New World prophets, to which they called all their contemporaries, as a road to salvation and to the discovery of the living God. Felipe Guamán Poma de Ayala (1534–1616), a Christian Quechua prophet, pointed out this route:

> This is why he made me poor, placing me among the rest of the poor, because it suited this purpose, since it is well known that the poor are despised by the rich and the haughty, who think that where the poor are

there is no God nor justice. Now we must realize clearly from our faith that where the poor are, there is Jesus Christ himself.[3]

Did anyone listen to this 'voice crying in the desert?' Like John the Baptist, and all the prophets, they often faced persecution, repression and death (Mark 6.17–29).

The first reaction was scandal and rejection. After the protest from Hispaniola in 1511, the authorities of the island, King Ferdinand V of Castile and the Dominican provincial, Alonso de Loaysa, criticized the condemnation. It had no theological basis, the king argued in his royal warrant of 20 March 1512. Bartolomé de Las Casas had to face increasing persecution, which did not even end with his death. In 1533 the Audience of Santo Domingo ordered him to retire to a monastery, and in 1548 Charles V ordered the withdrawal of his Confessional, which in some places had been burnt in public. His intransigence earned him the labels 'troublesome, inopportune, litigious and insulting' from the Franciscan Motolinia of Mexico. 'Rash, scandalous and a heretic,' he was called by the theologian Ginés de Sepúlveda in 1550. After his death Philip II in 1571 approved the measures taken by the viceroy of Peru, Francisco de Toledo, to confiscate the works of Las Casas.

Nevertheless, as early as 1517 his Dominican and Franciscan friends understood the persecution as a sign that he was following Jesus: 'If they persecuted me, they will persecute you too' (John 15.20).[4]

The bishops who followed Las Casas, the *lascasianos*, faced similar attacks to those on the prophet from Seville or worse. Fray Pablo de Torres, bishop of Panama between 1547 and 1554, was disowned by the local government, by the Council of the Indies and by his own archbishop, had to abandon his diocese, and was brought to Spain to face trial. Juan del Valle, bishop of Popayán between 1548 and 1560, had the strength to face the consequences of his option for the Indians: 'I am the worst bishop of the Indies in the opinion of the conquistadores,' he wrote in 1551. But, he added, 'If [the situation of the indigenous] does not improve, I shall speak out as usual, . . . even if they stone me, because these conquistadores resent these things so much that there would be no alternative.'[5] In 1558 he held a synod which condemned the effects of the invasion in such terms that the Crown refused to approve it. He was persecuted in Popayán, and received no support from the Royal Audience of Bogotá. Finally he tried to take the indigenous cause to the Council of Trent, but died on the journey to Europe. Fray Agustín de la Coruña, successor of Juan del Valle, bishop between 1565 and 1590, had to suffer incomprehension and exile. The Spaniards of his diocese disowned him as bishop, and the Audience of Quito imprisoned him unjustly between

1582 and 1587. Removed from his diocese, he complained in these terms to Philip II:

> Most Christian King, for having served you and preached obedience to your just laws. . . , do I deserve to be an exile? . . . [The Spaniards] are so hardened in so much cruelty that they do not regard it as sin, and say that in other parts there are bishops and Audiences and governors and preachers and orders, and they see this and say nothing, and only I protest.[6]

Fray Antonio de Valdiviesos, bishop of Nicaragua between 1544 and 1550, was stabbed to death on the orders of the powerful Contreras family, the main invaders of the area, on 26 February 1550.

In addition there was persecution of the many religious who sided with the Indians. Among many Franciscans we may mention Jerónimo de San Miguel in open conflict with the Audience of Bogotá, brought as a prisoner to Spain until 1552, and Alonso Maldonado de Buendía, imprisoned by the Inquisition in 1583 to silence his prophetic courage, which reached the ears of Pope Pius V.[7] Among the many Dominicans persecuted were Fray Tomás de Ortiz, protector of the Indians of Nueva Granada, who had to return to Spain in 1532, his mission a failure, and Fray Gil González de San Nicolás, founder of the Chilean Province, who, having to face persecution by the Inquisition and the attacks of the viceroy of Peru, had to leave Chile in 1563.

The prophets of the New World ended by sharing the fate of the victims of the invasion. They were also victims: 'Brother will betray brother, and a father his child . . . You will be universally hated on account of my name' (Mark 13.12–13).

The greatest humiliation in the world: an oppression greater than that of the people of God in Egypt, Babylon or Rome

The prophets of the sixteenth and seventeenth centuries insisted that what was happening in the Indies was less the construction or creation of a New World than the end of the indigenous world, a real end of the world, the destruction of the Indies, in Las Casas' accurate expression. It was what is considered today the greatest genocide in human history.[8]

One statement recurs like an echo in the words of these witnesses: the Indians are dying out. It was said in Venezuela, Chiapas, Tabasco, Oaxaca, Cartagena and Santiago de Chile. In Santiago Bishop Diego de Medellín wrote in 1587: 'All these natives are being so ill-treated and beaten so much, that is, those who live in peace, that if it continues they will die out.'[9] End of a world, death of a world.

Until the world ended, or until the Indians died out completely, the lament of the victims was to continue to be heard, and the prophet's duty was to bear witness to this, as Las Casas wrote about the tragedy of Moctezuma:

> This was something which threw all these kingdoms and peoples into grief and anguish and mourning and pain, and left them swollen with bitterness and pain, and from now to the end of the world, or they die out completely, they will not cease to lament and sing that calamity in their dances, as in romances (as we said above) . . .[10]

The voice of the prophets joined this elegiac song of the Indians, which was at the same time a cry for life and nothing more. The important 'Latin Letter from some Dominicans and Franciscans' written in Santo Domingo on 27 May 1517 is an example:

> The inhabitants of these islands are being destroyed and annihilated by violence, to such an extent that we can apply to them the passage from Isaiah, 'The highways lie waste, and the travellers are no more.' Their bodies are ill-treated with as much severity as the dung that is trodden into the ground . . . These people have been ill-treated to such a degree that their skin has stuck to their bones, and is dry.
>
> Impose no work on them . . . Be concerned solely for their lives and health, let them recover their strength and rest their weary bodies. Let them breathe and attempt to reproduce naturally. Time will show if something different and better can be done with them. For the present let this be our aim, that they should not disappear. They are dying in droves . . .

What sense can we make of this unheard-of violence in terms of the history of God's dealings with humankind? How are we to understand it in the light of the history of salvation?

The voices of those who spoke up for the victims read and re-read the Bible, and found a principle of comparison, which in the end showed that there was no comparison. The victims of the colonial invasion were being subjected to an oppression much greater than that suffered by the people of God in Egypt and Babylon, or even by the primitive church under Roman oppression. It was an incomprehensible injustice, which went beyond all known horizons, which leaped over the boundaries of the Bible!

Fray Pedro de Córdoba, vice-provincial of the Dominicans on Hispaniola, faces this problem in his letter to Charles V of 28 May 1517, in which he tries to measure the effects of the European invasion: 'I do not read or find that any nation, even among the infidel, has perpetrated so many evils and cruelties on their enemies in the style and manner in which Christians have done on these sad people who have been their friends and helpers in their own land . . .'[11]

The subject of violence against women, in particular, led Córdoba to claim that the Europeans were being responsible for an oppression greater than that suffered by Israel in Egypt: 'Women, whom all nations usually excuse from labour because of their weakness, in this land have worked and are still working as much as or more than men, and stripped and without food, without beds, like men, and some even pregnant or with newborn children – not even Pharaoh and the Egyptians inflicted such cruelty on the people of Israel.'

The comparison had been made. The 'Latin Letter' repeated the theme, and added another symbol, the persecution of the church by Rome:

> Reverend Sirs, where are the countless peoples discovered in this land, whose number the discoverers compared to the grass of the field? Of all these there remain on the island no more than ten or twelve thousand between men and women, and they broken and weakened, as it were, in their death agony . . . What famine fell on these people that wiped them off the face of the earth? Will no one remember them any more? Neither Pharaoh nor the people of Egypt ill-treated the children of Israel so cruelly, nor did the persecutors of the martyrs do so to the children of the church.

Other New World prophets, in different latitudes and at different times, took up this biblical comparison. Bishop Juan del Valle of Popayán, writing from Cali on 8 January 1551, as well as saying that the Indies seemed more like Babylon than Spanish territory, added that the indigenous people 'were more hard worked than the Israelites in Egypt'. In 1626 Bishop Francisco de Salcedo, of Santiago de Chile, having witnessed the oppression of the Guarpe Indians of Cuyo, denounced one even worse, widening the comparison to the Roman persecution of the church of the first centuries ('They bring them, perishing from thirst and hunger, with worse treatment than the Barbarian peoples gave to the Christians in the primitive church').[12]

Going a stage further, almost half a century later, in what was now a belated prophetic criticism, Fray Diego de Humanzoro issued a blazing denunciation of the situation of the Indians of Chile, and of the whole New World, calling it much worse than that of the Israelites in Israel or Babylon. Pleading before Queen Mariana of Austria in 1699, and with the authority of Las Casas, the Franciscan bishop said:

> The personal service of these Indians has always been, and still is, more intolerable than that of the children of Israel in Egypt and Babylon;

their slavery was very mild and gentle in comparison with what these miserable Indians have endured and still endure . . . In the slavery and tyranny of the Pharaohs of Egypt . . . they fell far short of exhaustion and death.

In four hundred years of captivity . . . the Hebrews increased in numbers and did not die. But our Indians in their own land, ever since the Spaniards entered it, have been wasted away in hundreds of millions by the harassment and tyranny they suffer, and by the severity of the personal sevice, which is greater and more terrible than that exacted by the Pharaohs of Egypt.[13]

The European invaders, representatives of Christ or Satan?

The discovery and conquest of the Indies were to reach their ultimate meaning as a force for the expansion of the gospel. The European presence in the New World brought about a universal victory of Christendom, an amazing spreading of Jesus Christ, as Columbus himself described it to Pope Alexander VI in 1502. The ideology of the age consisted in taking Christ to the barbarians and pagans caught up in the power of Satan. The colonial equation, God/Europe: Satan/Indies, formed the basis for the evangelization of the imperial churches on the new continent.

But the voices of those who were able to speak for the victims reversed this equation. They discovered, when they placed themselves in the places and eyes of the oppressed, that the Europeans were very often, in their actions, more like representatives of Satan than of Christ.

At the end of his treatise, *The Devastation of the Indies. A Brief Account*, Bartolomé de Las Casas told King Carlos V:

I, Fray Bartolomé de Las Casas or Casaus, friar of Santo Domingo . . . by the mercy of God am present at this Court, seeking to end the hell of the Indies . . .

What was this hell? It was the hell created by the Europeans in the New World, those who, like the Antichrist, '[do] not acknowledge Jesus Christ' (I John 4.3). It was 'those devils the landowners', who oppressed the Indians. When Las Casas described the exploitation of the Indians in the submarine pearl beds, he said, 'In this unbearable labour, or better, this task of hell, we have now killed all the Lucayan Indians' (B. de Las Casas, *Tratados*, pp. 113, 139, 189).

This historical and theological perception was shared by all the prophets of the New World. Bishop Juan Fernández de Angulo of Santa María (Colombia) denounced the invasion in 1540: 'There are no Christians, only demons.'[14] Francisco Nuñez de Pineda y Bascuñan (1608–1680), a

Creole and a layman from Chile who came to love the Mapuche, wrote of their forced evangelization: 'By force of arms and rough treatment they were made Christians, and became out of compliance and in name only, because [the Europeans] in words sought to appear ministers of Christ our Lord, and with their evil deeds were ambassadors and servants of Satan.'[15]

This attitude was a doubt and a challenge striking at the heart of the European presence in the Indies. Fray Diego de Humanzoro examined himself on this issue by the very words of Jesus. In 1669 he wrote to the Spanish court:

> Having discovered [the Indians] and added them to the Crown of Castile, as a reward for the religion and holiness of its glorious Majesties, we make bad use of the gift . . . so to say, the sins of our bad example, greed and inhumanity . . . which give foreigners an opportunity to use to us those hard and fearful words which Christ used to the scribes and Pharisees, quoted in St Matthew, Chapter 23: 'Alas for you, scribes and Pharisees, you hypocrites! You travel over land and sea to make a single proselyte, and anyone who becomes one you make twice as fit for hell as you are.'

The enterprise of the Indies is diabolical: 'There are many deceivers at large in the world, refusing to acknowledge Jesus Christ as coming in human nature. They are the Deceiver; they are the Antichrist' (II John 7). Over the New World there hung a very great tribulation, the false and deceptive appearance of Christianity, which could only be dispelled by a renewed manifestation of the justice of God for the poor.

This was the voice of the Mayan prophets – are we to call them Christian? – or Chilam Balam de Chumayel, who devastatingly revealed the truth of all the prophets of the New World after the conquest:

> It was only because of the mad time, the mad priests, that sadness came among us, that Christianity came among us; for the great Christians came here with the true God; but that was the beginning of our distress, the beginning of the tribute, the beginning of the alms, what made the hidden discord appear,
> the beginning of the fighting with firearms, . . .
> The poor people did not protest against what they felt a slavery,
> the Antichrist on earth, tiger of the peoples,
> wildcat of the peoples, sucking the Indian people dry.
> But the day will come when the tears of their eyes reach God and God's justice
> comes down and strikes the world.[16]

Translated by Francis McDonagh

Notes

1. Cf. Enrique Dussel, *El episcopado latinoamericano y la liberación de los pobres 1504–1620*, Mexico 1979, p. 103.
2. Fernando Aliaga, *Relaciones a la Santa Sede enviadas por los obispos de Chile colonial, Anales de la Facultad de Teología*, XXV, 1, 1974, Santiago de Chile, 62.
3. Quoted in Gustavo Gutiérrez, *Dios o el oro en las Indias (siglo XVI)*, Lima 1989, p. 171. On the Quechua prophet, see Rolena Adorno, *Guamán Poma. Writing and Resistance in Colonial Peru*, Austin, Texas 1986.
4. *Carta latina de dominicos y franciscanos a los gobernadores de los reinos de España*, Santa Domingo, 27 May 1517, in: *Casas Reales* 18 (1988), Museo de las Casas Reales, Dominican Republic, 66–70.
5. Dussel, *Episcopado* (n. 1), p. 351.
6. Ibid., p. 359. The author concludes that Philip II 'morally murdered' the prophet from Popayán.
7. Mariano Errasti, *América franciscana. Evangelizadores e indigenistas franciscanos del siglo XVI*, Santiago de Chile, pp. 253–63, 309–16.
8. Tzvetan Todorov, *La conquista de América. La cuestión del otro*, Mexico 1987, p. 14.
9. Letter from Fray Diego de Medellín to Philip II, Santiago, 17 January 1587, in: *Colección de Documentos Históricos del Archivo del Arzobispado de Santiago*, Santiago 1919, vol. I, p. 33.
10. B. de Las Casas, *Tratados*, Mexico 1974, p. 73.
11. Letter of Fr Fray Pedro de Córdoba to King Charles V, Santo Domingo, Hispaniola, 28 May 1517. Cf. M. A. Medina, *Una comunidad al servicio del indio. La obra de Fr. Pedro de Córdoba OP*, Madrid 1983.
12. Edict of Francisco de Salcedo, bishop of Santiago de Chile, on the Guarpe Indians, Santiago, 16 May 1626, in: *Colección de Documentos Históricos del Archivo del Arzobispado de Santiago*, Santiago 1919, vol. I, p. 120.
13. Letter of Fray Diego de Humanzoro to Queen Mariana of Austria, Santiago, 4 July 1669, in *Archivo del Arzobispado de Santiago*, vol. I, pp. 299–300.
14. Dussel, *Episcopado* (n. 1), p. 96.
15. Francisco Nuñez de Pineda, *Cautiverio feliz*, a work written in 1673 and dedicated to King Charles II, in: *Colección de Historiadores de Chile*, vol. III, p. 326.
16. Cf. Miguel León-Portilla, *El reverso de la conquista*, Mexico 1964, p. 86.

III · The Life Power of the Cross

With the Eyes of a European Theologian

Johann Baptist Metz

I would like to subject my contribution to the quincentenary to the criterion of a personal recollection: that of my experiences in Latin America in 1988. Of course I have to be selective, and in turn this selection is necessarily subjective. My memories are continually far more besieged by faces than by ideas, than by what I heard and read. My strongest, most disquieting recollections are of the faces in Latin America.

I

'Come right up to the balustrade,' said Bishop Murelli to me during a liturgy in Caxia. 'Come up so that you can see the faces.' They were above all, time and again, small faces, black faces, faces which shone – for moments, for a song, for the duration of a cry, a shout. And there were dreams, there were desires in these eyes – or also tears.

Then I saw the other faces, the other eyes: among the *campesinos* eking out the most wretched of existences round the edges of Lima, above all, time and again, among the poor women, and above all – particularly at night – among the street children of São Paulo. I saw the eyes without dreams, the faces without tears, as it were the unhappiness beyond wishing. I saw children's faces, deadened as a result of sniffing a disgusting glue – as a substitute for opium, the substitute for dreams in a life which is truly forced below the level of dreams, below the limits of tears: poverty, which ends up in the wretchedness of being without dreams or tears! Those of whom I am speaking are not sixty or seventy years old, with burnt out, used up dreams; they are three, five years of age, street children with no parents and no one to care for them – and how many of these hundreds of thousands would still be alive if I were to go back?

And finally I kept seeing the faces of the Indians, faces shaped by the dark shadows of what is called the mysticism of the Andes. At all events, I, the European, would call it a kind of mysticism of mourning. There is constitutional mourning in the Andes. However, among these Indians, faces have long been in process of modernization. If you spend too long looking at television, your face changes. Will this mourning prove capable of being combined with our Western civilization? Or will we simply develop the Indians out of their mourning? In my view, were that to happen, humankind would be poorer by a hope. I don't want to romanticize. There is nothing romantic about these mourning faces of the Indians, and in any case 'romantic' is far too European a category: it is in fact a favourite term of disparagement used by those who do not want to concede our own inability to mourn. In my view these mourning faces are shaped by a distinctive strength, a secret resistance. Against what? Against the hectic acceleration of time, which we have brought about and to which we ourselves have long been subjected? Against the forgetfulness that nests in our modern consciousness? These faces seem to be missing something that we have long forgotten in the name of 'progress' and 'development'. Christian hope is certainly no kind of superficial optimism. The substance of Christian hope is not simply remote from mourning, stripped of any kind of mourning. With the inability to mourn there ultimately develops an inability to allow oneself to be comforted and to understand or experience any comfort other than mere postponement.

II

Can we Christians here in Europe, can the churches of our country, bear to look at these faces? Can we, do we want to, risk the change of perspective and see our lives as Christians, in the churches – at least for a moment – from the perspective of these faces? Or do we experience and define ourselves exclusively with our backs to such faces? The temptation to do that is great and, unless I am mistaken, it is growing. 1992: who among us does not think primarily of the Single European Market and the new possibilities for trading which have meanwhile opened up to it in Central and Eastern Europe? And if we in Europe associate 1992 with Columbus, with the quincentenary of his discovery (1492–1992), do we not do so exclusively from our perspective? Does not a crypto-triumphalism prevent us honestly from adopting any other perspective?

Such questions become more acute when one notes the mentality which (in my view) is at present to be found in Europe (and in North America) and which is spreading. By way of a definition I might venture to call it the 'everyday postmodernism' of our hearts, which is again putting the so-called Third World at a faceless distance. Is there not at present something like a cultural and spiritual strategy of immunizing Europe, a tendency towards a mental isolationism, the cult of a new innocence, an attempt intellectually to avoid the global demands made on us, a new variant of what I once called 'tactical provincialism'? What can be described philosophically as post-modern thought – the repudiation of universalist categories, thinking 'in differences', in diminished numbers, in colourful fragments – has a parallel in everyday life. Is there not a new mood among us which is again putting the distress and wretchedness of the poor peoples at a greater existential distance from us? Is not a new provincialism spreading among us, a new form of privatization of our lives, the mentality of an onlooker without any obligation to critical perception, a voyeuristic approach to the great situations of crisis and suffering in the world? In our Enlightened European world are there not increasing indications of a new, as it were secondary, innocence which is nourished by the impression that while nowadays we are more informed than ever about everything, above all about what threatens us, and about all the crises and terrors in the world, the move from knowledge to action, from information to support, was never so great and so unlikely as it is today? And does not such an impression dispose one to resignation? Or to a flight into myth and its dreams of innocence, remote from action? Is not an over-familiarity with crises and misery rife among us? In the end we get used to the crises over poverty in the world which seem increasingly to be a permanent part of the scene, so that we shrug our shoulders and delegate them to an anonymous social evolution which has no subjects.

However, for the church, the sorry reality of these poor lands which cries out to heaven has long become been a fateful question, a touchstone of its character as a world church. In the end of the day the church does not only 'have' a Third World church; by now it 'is' largely a Third World church, with a history of European origins with which it cannot dispense. In view of the mass misery which cries out to heaven (or no longer cries out because its language and dreams have long been shattered), the church cannot reassure itself that here it is experiencing the tragedies of a time-shift in a world which is coming together with increasing rapidity. Nor can it tell itself that these poor are the victims or even the hostages of their own heartless oligarchies. The world church needs to spell out and take seriously what was said biblically in the language of an archaic itinerant Christianity preached round the villages: 'What you did to the least . . .'

The European church may not, therefore, as it were in a post-modern way, allow its criteria to be talked out or belittled under the pressure of circumstances and mentalities. It may not withdraw from the tension between mysticism and politics into a thinking in terms of myths which is remote from history. In the end, with its creed 'suffered under Pontius Pilate', it is and remains attached to concrete history, to that history in which there is crucifixion, torture, suffering, hatred, weeping – and loving. No myth can give it back that innocence which it loses in such a history.

Certainly the church is not primarily a moral institution, but the bearer of a hope. And its theology is not primarily an ethic but an eschatology. But the roots of its power lie precisely in the helplessness of not giving up the criteria of responsibility and solidarity and leaving the preferential option to the poor only to the poor churches. All this has to do with the greatness and the burden which is laid on us with the biblical word 'God'. It does not remove us from social and political life, but simply takes away the basis of hatred and violence from this life. And it calls on all men and women to walk upright, so that all can kneel voluntarily and give thanks with gladness.

III

Once again the faces, and even more the eyes. With what eyes was Latin America, was this 'Catholic continent', discovered? At the beginning of the times which in Europe we call 'modern', at the beginning of the modern period, an anthropology of domination was developing – secretly, and overlaid by many religious and cultural symbols. Man understood himself increasingly as a dominant subject, there to put nature under his control. His identity was formed by this lordly subjection, this seizing of power over nature. His eyes looked downwards. His logic became a logic of domination, not of recognition: at all events a logic of assimilation and not of otherness. All virtues which did not contribute to domination – friendliness and gratitude, a capacity for suffering and sympathy, mourning and tenderness – faded into the background, were cognitively depotentiated or at all events entrusted to the world of women in a treacherous 'division of labour'. We may have long failed to notice the features of this anthropology and logic of domination because the pressure towards subjection very soon shifted outwards – against alien minorities, alien races and alien cultures. Obviously the history of European colonization has its roots here. And who would venture to dispute that this mechanism of domination continually made its way through into the history of Christian mission as well?

Certainly, the project of European modernity contributed, and continues to contribute, quite different features. Thus within it – in the processes of political Enlightenment – there developed a reason which seeks to be practical in achieving freedom and justice. For a long time it was encoded in European terms. So what came about in the meanwhile was a developing 'secular' Europeanization of the world – by way of science, technology and economics; in short by way of the world-domination of Western rationality. However, this caught up the whole world in a tremendous frenzy of acceleration. The dawn of the industrial age already brought with it great impoverishment and misery in Europe, especially in the last century. Although the pace of this European industrial development has been quite rapid, and Europe has changed more in the last 150 years than in the whole of the past 2000, among us the development nevertheless took place in slow motion compared with the pace of the process of industrialization that can be noted, for example, in Brazil. The growing acceleration of this modernization, this industrial and technical development – above all in post-urban metropolises like São Paulo – seems to be matched by an increase in impoverishment which has grown exponentially. The development has no time to develop. It destroys the time of human beings, who seem to be crushed between pre-modern conditions of life and rule and post-modern technology.

The political culture which seeks freedom and justice for all can be established only if among us and in those Latin American countries it is combined with another culture which, for want of a better term, I might call a new hermeneutical culture: the culture of the recognition of others in their otherness, with the way in which they form a social and cultural identity, with their own images of hope and recollection. It is imperative that supposedly neutral economic and technological forces which are allegedly free of political and moral pressures should be tested by them. Only such a culture of recognition makes possible a respectable and redemptive interchange between Europe and these countries. Indeed in the end the European spirit is itself endangered by the process of modernization which it has set in motion: it increasingly acts as an automatic process, and increasingly human beings in these processes are merely their own experiments, and less and less their memories.

IV

From the very beginning, with its consciousness of mission Christianity struggled for a culture of the recognition of the other. What was to be normative for this consciousness of mission was not Hellenistic thinking in terms of identity and assimilation, but the biblical notion of the covenant, according to which it is not like that is known by like but, rather, unlikes know one another by recognizing one another. One example of this is the dispute between Peter and Paul along with the dispute at the Apostolic Council over the question whether Gentile Christians were to be circumcised. This recognition of the others in their otherness is expressed in the refusal of the Jewish Christian Paul to subject the Gentile Christians to circumcision. So at the roots of the biblical tradition lie the impulses to a new hermeneutical culture: any 'will to power' is really alien to it, in the recognition of the others in their otherness. This hermeneutical culture was again obscured in the history of Europe; it also faded into the background in the history of the church. So with what eyes was the Latin American continent 'discovered'? Did this early Christian hermeneutic of recognition play a normative role? Or was the process of the Christianization of America not far more (if not exclusively) accompanied by a questionable hermeneutic of assimilation, a hermeneutic of domination, which had no eyes for the trace of God in the otherness of the others and which therefore continually also violated the culture of these others which it did not understand, and made them victims? At any rate we must use this question to measure all the ceremonial words which are spoken on the occasion of the quincentenary.

V

The church does not hope for itself. Therefore it does not need to split its own history – in a suspiciously ideological fashion – in order only to display the sunny side of this history, as those must do who 'have no hope'. To concede failure does not mean falling into a neurotically arrogant cult of self-accusation. It is quite simply a matter of honouring our eschatological hope and venturing conversion and new ways in the light of it.

That also applies, *mutatis mutandis*, to our Christian theology. I have often asked myself why so little attention is paid to the history of human suffering. Is that the sign of a particularly strong faith? Or is it perhaps just the expression of a historical way of thinking, detached from any situation and empty of humanity, a kind of idealism which is equipped with a high degree of apathy in the face of the catastrophes and downfalls of others? The new political theology in Europe developed, among other things, out of the attempt to make the cry of the victims of Auschwitz unforgettable in the *logos* of theology. And the theological impetus of liberation theology, as I understand it, comes from the attempt to make it possible to hear the cry of the poor in the *logos* of theology and make the face of strange other men and women recognizable in it, i.e. to interrupt the flood of ideas and the closed character of systematic argumentation with this cry and with these faces. That may make the language of theology small, poor and completely unsolemn. But if it becomes that, it will come close to its original task. In the end the mysticism which Jesus lived out and taught and which should also have directed the *logos* of Christian theology is not a narrow mysticism of closed eyes, but an empathetic mysticism of opened eyes (cf. e.g. Luke 10.25–37). The God of Jesus cannot be found either here or there if we ignore its perceptions.

The Crucified Peoples: Yahweh's Suffering Servant Today

In Memory of Ignacio Ellacuría[1]

Jon Sobrino

Ignacio Ellacuría admired Jürgen Moltmann's well-known book *The Crucified God*, but he made a point of stressing another much more urgent theological idea: *the crucified people*. This was not just for historical reasons (our reality is like this), but also for theological ones (God's creation is like this). It is necessary for us to speak of these crucified peoples in relation to 1992, as well, in order to recall their historical causes. And the sole object of all this talk must be to bring them down from the cross.

I. The crucified peoples: a horrifying fact

The obvious is the least obvious, Ellacuría used to say. And this is our starting point for talking about the crucified peoples. When what is obvious 'in others' – the crucified peoples – shows us what 'we' are, we tend to ignore it, cover it up or distort it because it simply terrifies us. So it is understandable that we should ignore the evidence of the crucified peoples, but we must at least suspect – especially in the Western world, which boasts it has been schooled by the great masters of suspicion – that this ignorance is not mere ignorance, but a will to ignore and cover up. So let us start by dis-covering the covered-up reality of our world.

That creation has turned out badly for God – another provocative phrase of Ignacio Ellacuría's – is confirmed by economists. Terrible poverty is increasing in Latin America. It is estimated that by the end of the century some 170 million Latin Americans will be living in dire poverty and another 170 million in poverty critical to life. And to this inhuman poverty we must add the victims of repression and the wars it has caused. In

Central America alone the victims are estimated to be a quarter of a million.

The Latin American bishops have said so. What characterizes Latin America is 'the misery that marginalizes large human groups' which 'as a collective fact is an injustice crying to heaven', (Medellín, *Justicia*, no. 1, 1968), 'the situation of inhuman poverty in which millions of Latin Americans live' (Puebla, no. 29, 1979). And John-Paul II repeated it again in *Sollicitudo rei socialis* (1987).

Whether we look at it from the worldly or the Christian point of view, both agree about the tragedy. Looking at the present situation, which we can see and touch in one way or another, helps us to grasp what happened centuries ago. At the origin of what we call Latin America today there lies an original and originating sin. To give one single fact: some seventy years after 1492 the indigenous population had been reduced to 15%; many of their cultures had been destroyed and subjected to anthropological death. This was a colossal disaster, doubtless due to various complex causes, but nevertheless a really colossal disaster. 'For some time . . . I have felt the disappearance of whole peoples as an absurd mystery of historical iniquity, which reduces me to the most abject sort of faith', says Casadáliga.[2]

So there was a historical disaster and we have to give it a name. Our current language calls these peoples 'Third World', 'the South', 'developing countries' . . . These designations are attempting to say that something is wrong, but such language does not communicate *how* wrong. Therefore we need to speak of crucified peoples: metaphorical language, of course, but language which conveys much better than others the historical enormity of the disaster and its meaning for faith. At any rate, it is much better at avoiding the cover-up operated by other languages.

'Crucified peoples' is useful and necessary language at the real level of fact, because 'cross' means death and death is what the Latin American peoples are subjected to in thousands of ways. It is slow but real death caused by the poverty generated by unjust structures – 'institutionalized violence': 'the poor are those who die before their time'. It is swift violent death, caused by repression and wars, when the poor threaten these unjust structures. And it is indirect but effective death when peoples are deprived even of their cultures in order to weaken their identities and make them more defenceless.

It is useful and necessary language at the historical-ethical level because 'cross' expresses a type of death actively inflicted. To die crucified does not mean simply to die, but to be put to death; it means that there are victims and there are executioners. It means that there is a very grave sin. The crucified peoples do not fall from heaven – if we followed the metaphor through we should have to say that they rise from hell. However much people try to soften the fact, the truth is that the Latin American peoples' cross has been inflicted on them by the various empires that have taken power over the continent: the Spanish and Portuguese yesterday, the US and its allies today; whether by armies or economic systems, or the imposition of cultures and religious views, in connivance with the local powers.

It is useful and necessary language at the religious level because 'cross' – Jesus suffered death on the cross and not any other death – evokes sin and grace, condemnation and salvation, human action and God's action. From a Christian point of view God himself makes himself present in these crosses, and the crucified peoples become the principal sign of the times. 'This sign' (of God's presence in our world) 'is always the historically crucified people.'[3]

Crucified peoples exist. It is necessary and urgent to see our world this way. And it is right to call them this because this language stresses their historical tragedy and their meaning for faith.

II. The crucified people as Yahweh's suffering servant

In Latin America the fundamental theological statement affirms that the crucified people are the actualization of Christ crucified, the true servant of Yahweh; the crucified people and Christ, Yahweh's servant, refer to and explain each other. This is what two Salvadoran martyrs did, who knew very well what they were talking about. Monseñor Romero told some terrorized peasants who had survived a massacre, 'You are the image of the divine victim',[4] and in another sermon he said that Jesus Christ, the liberator, is so closely identified with the people that interpreters of scripture cannot tell whether Yahweh's servant proclaimed by Isaiah is the suffering people or Christ who comes to redeem us.[5] Ellacuría said the same: 'This crucified people is the historical continuation of Yahweh's servant, whom the sin of the world continues to deprive of any human decency, and from whom the powerful of this world continue to rob everything, taking everything away, even life, especially life.'[6]

This theology of the crucified people has become established in Latin America, whereas in other places it may seem exaggerated, unjustified or unscientific pious language. This is because hermeneutics seeks not only common horizons of cultural understanding between the present and the past, but above all common horizons of reality. This common reality appears clearly in Latin America. The theology of the crucified people as Yahweh's suffering servant includes not only the servant as victim – which people in other situations can understand – but also the servant's saving role in history: historical soteriology, as Ignacio Ellacuría insisted, which is more alien to the theologies of other latitudes and difficult even to imagine if the reality is not seen.

However, to grasp this theology, we need only read the songs of Yahweh's servant with the text in one hand and our eyes on the crucified peoples. So let us do this in the form of a meditation.[7]

What do the songs say about the servant? Above all he is a 'man of sorrows acquainted with grief', and this is the normal condition of the crucified people: hunger, sickness, slums, frustration through lack of education, health, employment . . . And if their penalties are innumerable in normal times, 'peace time', as it is called, they increase even more when, like the servant, they decide to 'establish justice and right'. Then repression falls on them and the verdict 'guilty of death'. Massacres occur, as at Sumpul and El Mozote in El Salvador or Huehuetenango in Guatemala and so many other places. The people become even more like the servant with 'no form or comeliness . . . no beauty'. And to the ugliness of daily poverty is added that of disfiguring bloodshed, the terror of tortures and mutilations. Then, like the servant, they arouse revulsion: 'many were frightened by him because he was disfigured and did not seem to be a man or look like a human being'. And people 'hide their faces from him,' because they are disgusted, and also so as not to disturb the false happiness of those responsible for the servant, or unmask the truth hidden behind the euphemisms we invent daily to describe him.

Like the servant, the crucified people are 'despised and rejected'; everything has been taken from them, even human dignity. And really what can the world learn and receive from them? What do they offer the world for its progress, apart from their primary materials, their beaches and volcanoes, their folklore for tourists? They are not respected but despised. And this contempt reaches its height when ideology takes on a religious tinge to condemn them in God's name. It is said of the servant: 'We esteemed him stricken, smitten by God, counted among the sinners.' And what is said about the crucified peoples? As long as they suffer patiently, they are regarded as having a certain goodness, simplicity, piety especially, which is unenlightened and superstitious, but none-the-less surprises the educated and secularized people from other worlds. Yet when they decide to live and call on God to defend them and set them free, then they are not even recognized as God's people, and the well-known litany is intoned: they are subversives, terrorists, criminals, atheists, Marxists and Communists. Despised and murdered in life, they are also despised in death. It is said of the servant: 'They made his grave with the wicked and his tomb with evildoers.' This is also the crucified people's epitaph. And sometimes they do not even have this, because though ancient piety denied no one a grave, the crucified people sometimes do not even have this. This is what happens to the disappeared: corpses thrown on rubbish tips, clandestine cemeteries.

It is said of the servant that 'he was oppressed and he was afflicted yet he opened not his mouth', that he died in total meekness. Today not all the crucified die like this. Monseñor Romero was able to speak in his lifetime and his death shook many consciences. So did the death of priests and nuns, and recently that of Ignacio Ellacuría and the other five Jesuits in the UCA. But who knows the seventy thousand assassinated in El Salvador and the eighty thousand in Guatemala? What word is uttered by the children of Ethiopia and the three hundred million in India living in dire poverty? There are thousands and millions who do not say a word. It is not known how they live or how they died. Their names are not known – Julia Elba and Celina are known because they were murdered with the Jesuits. Even their number is not known.

Finally it is said of the servant that 'he was taken away defenceless and without judgment' in total impotence against arbitrary injustice. Again this does not apply altogether to the crucified people. Many fight for their lives and there is no lack of prophets to defend them. But the repression against their struggle is brutal: first they try to discredit the prophets and then co-opt them for a civil and ecclesiastical society that presents them as tokens of freedom and democracy – with well calculated risks – until they become really dangerous. Then they kill them too. Is there a real court to defend the cause of the poor, that at least listens to them and does them justice? No serious notice is taken of them during their lives, and when they die their deaths are not even investigated.

The crucified people are this suffering servant of Yahweh today. This fact is covered up, because like the servant, the people are innocent: 'He had done no violence and there was no deceit in his mouth.' The servant not only proclaims the truth of the crucified people, but also the truth about their killers. All of us can and must look at ourselves reflected in the crucified people in order to grasp our deepest reality. As in a mirror, we can see what we are by what we produce.

And we have to be very aware of this in 1992. Some will recall the advances in science and democracy that the Western world has brought, and the church will remember the preaching of the gospel. Others will add that things are not as simple as that, that we cannot blame others entirely for the crucifixion. But at the hour of truth, unless we profoundly accept the truth of the crucified peoples and the fundamental responsibility of successive empires for their crucifixion, we will miss the main fact. That is, that in this world there is still enormous sin; sin is what killed the servant – the Son of God – and sin is what continues to kill God's children. And this sin is inflicted by some upon others. In a typically Spanish turn of phrase

Ellacuría summed up what successive empires have done to the Latin American continent: 'they have left it like a Christ' – they have made a Christ of it.[8]

III. The salvation the crucified peoples bring

The foregoing theology is fundamental, and to some extent it is usually adopted in other theologies, especially as an expression of the current problem of theodicy, 'how to do theology after Auschwitz'. However, in Latin America, we add a second perspective belonging more specifically to liberation theology: we must bring the crucified peoples down from the cross. This is the requirement of an anthropodicy by which human beings can be justified. This can only be done by bringing the crucified peoples down from their crosses.

This is the marrow of liberation theology. And what we want to stress now is that the crucified people themselves are bearers of salvation. The one chosen by God to bring salvation is the servant, which increases the scandal. We sincerely believe that theology does not know what to do with this central statement, unless it seeks in the servant's 'vicarious expiation' a theoretical model for understanding Christ's redemption on the cross. But this model does not illuminate what salvation the cross brings, far less what historical salvation the cross brings today. Yet if we abandoned the salvation brought by the servant we would be throwing out something central in the faith. Liberation theology has tried to analyse what salvation and what historical salvation is brought by the servant, and Ellacuría did so with great rigour and vigour in his work *The Crucified People*, which he subtitled 'an essay in historical soteriology'. Understanding what salvation is brought by the crucified people's suffering is not only or principally a matter of speculation and interpretation of texts. It is a matter of grasping the reality.

The light the crucified peoples bring

God says of the servant that he will set him up as a 'light for the nations' (Isa. 42.6; 49.6). Today this light is to show the nations what they really are. Which is no small benefit. Imprisoning the truth by injustice is the fundamental sin of individuals and also of the nations. Many evils derive from it: among others, the darkening of the heart. A light whose power is capable of unmasking lies is very beneficial and very necessary. This is the light offered by the crucified people. If the first world cannot see its own reality in this light, we do not know what can make it do so.

Ellacuría expressed this graphically in various ways. He said bluntly, using a medical metaphor, that in order to test the health of the First World it was necessary to do a 'coproanalysis', that is, to examine its faeces. Because it is the reality of the crucified peoples that appears in that analysis, and their reality reveals that of those who produce them.

He also said that the Third World offers a great advantage over the First World in throwing light on where we ought to be going:

> From my viewpoint – and this can be one that is both prophetic and paradoxical at once – the US is much worse off than Latin America. Because the US has a solution but in my opinion it is a bad solution, both for them and for the world as a whole. On the other hand, in Latin America there are no solutions, there are only problems. But however painful it is, it is better to have problems than to have a wrong solution for the future of history.[9]

The solution offered by the First World today is factually wrong, because it is unreal; it is not universalizable. And it is ethically wrong because it is dehumanizing for all, for them and for the Third World.

Finally he said that the Third World offered light on what historical utopia must be today. Utopia in the world today can only be a 'civilization of poverty',[10] all sharing austerely in the earth's resources so that they stretch to everybody. And this 'sharing' achieves what the First World does not offer: fellowship and, with it, meaning to life. He proposed as the way to reach this utopia a civilization of labour as against the current civilization of capital, in all its capitalist and socialist forms.

This is the light given by the crucified peoples. If it is allowed to shine, 1992 will be a very beneficial year. Undoubtedly it will produce panic and disruption, but the light will also dispel the darkness and heal. Instead of the 'discovery of America' we shall see the 'cover-up' that has been done there, and that what 1492 discovered was above all the reality of the Spanish and Portuguese empire at the time and the Catholic church at the time: a tragic but fruitful discovery. It will also produce the light of utopia: that true progress cannot consist in what is offered now, but in bringing the crucified peoples down from the cross and sharing the resources and everybody's goods with all.

The salvation the crucified peoples bring

The crucified peoples also offer positive salvation. Obviously, this is scandalous, but unless we accept it in principle, it will be pointless to repeat that there is salvation in the servant, that the crucified Christ has taken upon himself and got rid of the sin of the world. What we have to do is verify this salvation historically.

Above all the crucified peoples offer values that are not offered elsewhere. We may discuss whether they create these values because they have nothing else to hold on to, and whether these values will disappear when their present economic and social circumstances disappear and are devoured by the western capitalist world and its 'civilization'. But they are there now and are offered to all (and those who work to bring the people down from the cross also work to prevent these values disappearing).

Puebla said it with chilling clarity, although Western countries and churches have taken very little notice: the poor have evangelizing potential. This potential is spelt out as 'the gospel values of solidarity, service, simplicity and readiness to receive God's gift' (no. 1147). In historical language, the poor have a humanizing potential because they offer community against individualism, co-operation against selfishness, simplicity against opulence and openness to transcendence against blatant positivism, so prevalent in the civilization of the Western world. It is true, of course, that not all the poor offer this, but it is also true that they do offer it and, structurally speaking, in a form not offered by the First World.

The crucified peoples also offer hope, foolish or absurd, it might be said; because it is the only thing they have left, others argue. But once again, it is there, and it must not be trivialized by other worlds. That it is hope against hope is obvious, but it is also active hope that has shown itself in work and liberation struggles. What success these have is another matter, and the Western world appears to emerge triumphant and suffocate them all. But we should not hail this as a triumph but mourn it as a disaster, because it is crushing the hope of the poor and thus depriving itself of their humanizing potential. In any case, the very fact that hope arises and re-arises in history shows that history has a current of hope running through it which is available to all. The bearers of this current of hope are the crucified peoples.

The crucified peoples offer great love. It is not masochism or an invitation to suicide, nor making a virtue of necessity, but it is simply true that Latin America's innumerable martyrs show that love is possible because it is real, and great love is possible because many have shown it. And in a structurally selfish world based on selfishness and making a virtue of it – not in so many words of course – that love is a great offer of humanization.

The crucified peoples are ready to forgive their oppressors. They do not want to triumph over them but to share with them. To those who come to help them, they open their arms and accept them and thus, even without knowing it themselves, they forgive them. In this way they introduce into the Western world that reality which is so humanizing and so lacking, which is gratuitousness: not only what you get for yourself, but also what you are given unexpectedly, freely and without having to earn it.

The crucified peoples have generated solidarity: human beings and Christians mutually supporting one another, in this way and that, open to one another, giving and receiving one another's best. This solidarity is small, quantitatively speaking; it is only between church and human groups. But we must stress that now it is real and that it did not exist before. On a small scale it offers a model of how people and churches can relate to one another in a human and Christian way.

Finally, the crucified peoples offer faith, a way of being the church and a more genuine, Christian and relevant holiness for the world today, that gives more of Jesus. Again, this is more like a seed than a leafy tree, but it is there. And we cannot see any other faith, any other way of being the church, or any other holiness that humanizes humanity any better, or is a better way of bringing it to God.

It is paradoxical, but it is true. The crucified peoples offer light and salvation. Both can be had in 1992 by those who declare themselves their discoverers, although they have mostly been their coverers-up. Not to receive them would be ungrateful and idiotic; it would be the most radical way of ruining the 1992 'celebrations'. Receiving them and letting this gift become a new impulse to bring the people down from the cross would be the best – and the only – proper celebration. Liberated and given grace by the crucified peoples, the First World could become grace and liberation for them. And then there really will be something to 'celebrate': solidarity of human beings, mutually supporting one another, universal fellowship.

I wish to end with the words with which Ignacio Ellacuría concluded his reflections on 1992. He was not in the least inclined to ahistorical idealism or purely transcendental statements that could not be located in history.

I wish to state the following. Far from causing discouragement and despair, all this martyr's blood spilt in El Salvador and the whole of Latin America infuses our people with a new spirit of struggle and new hope. In this sense, if we are not a 'new world' or a 'new continent', we are clearly and demonstrably a continent of hope, which is a highly interesting symptom of a future new relation to other continents which do not have hope – the only thing they really have is fear.[11]

Translated by Dinah Livingstone

Notes

1. I dedicate this article to Ignacio Ellacuría because he dedicated his life to the

crucified people and in his death assumed their fate. He also made them the object of his theological reflection. See his article written in 1978: 'El Pueblo crucificado. Ensayo de soterología histórica', *Revista Latinoamerica de Teología* 18, 1989, pp. 305–33, and 'Discernir "el signo" de los tiempos', *Diakonía* 17, 1981, pp. 57–9. On 1992 he wrote *Quinto Centenario. América Latina. ¿Descubrimiento o encubrimiento?*, Barcelona 1990.

2. 'The "Crucified" Indians – A Case of Anonymous Collective Martyrdom'. *Concilium* 163, 1983, p. 51.

3. Ellacuría, 'Discernir' (n. 1), p. 58.

4. *La Voz de los sin Voz*, San Salvador 1980, p. 208.

5. Ibid., p. 366.

6. Ellacuría, 'Discernir' (n. 1), p. 58.

7. Here I repeat much of what was said in 'Meditación ante el pueblo crucificado', *Sal Terrae* 2, 1986, pp. 93–104; 'Brief an Ludwig Kaufmann aus El Salvador', in *Bioteppe der Hoffnung*, Olten & Freiburg im Breisgau 1988, pp. 392–8. See also *The Crucified Peoples* (CIIR pamphlet), London 1989.

8. *Quinto Centenario* (n. 1), p. 11.

9. Ibid.

10. 'The Kingdom of God and Unemployment in the Third World', *Concilium* 180, 1982, pp. 91–6.

11. *Quinto Centenario* (n. 1), p. 16.

The New Evangelization: New Life Bursts In

Leonardo Boff

The first evangelization of Latin America took place under the sign of subjection, because it took shape as part of the project of invasion and colonization. It gave rise to a colonized Christianity, which reproduced the religious models of the Iberian centres. From its very beginnings it was contradictory, because alongside the political and religious domination there were always prophetic spirits who denounced and resisted the perverse nature of the colonization in the name of the humanitarian spirit and liberating content of the Christian message, defending the Indians and condemning the evil of slavery.

The new evangelization puts down roots in this prophetic and pastoral tradition. It is taking place under the sign of liberation. It is giving rise to a unique Christianity, bearing the stamp of the ordinary people, brown, white, Latin, indigenous and black, pointing the way to new forms of church structure and also one of the forces for social change on the continent.

I. In what sense is this evangelization new?

Evangelization always occurs in a process of encounter between a given historical society and the Christian message. Puebla, in 1979, correctly traced for us the path of any evangelization worthy of the name:

> The church has been acquiring an increasingly clear and deep realization that evangelization is its fundamental mission; and that it cannot possibly carry out this mission without an ongoing effort to know the real situation and to adapt the gospel message to today's human beings in a dynamic, attractive and convincing way (85).

The premise of this statement is as follows: the good news is the result of a confrontation between a given historical and social situation, with its contradictions and potentialities, and Jesus' offer. What makes it good news is not simply the fact that the gospel is preached, but its capacity to transform a situation that is bad, inhuman and oppressive into one which is liberated, human and good. When this occurs, there is evangelization, and the message of Jesus is alive in the way people act.

The lives of the peoples of Latin America are imbued with vast hopes emerging out of a sea of oppressions: oppressed cultures, humiliated races, exploited classes. The social fabric of Latin America is being torn from top to bottom. Confronting this anti-life we find a mobilization of the oppressed, who, in a thousand different ways, are becoming aware, organizing, resisting and trying to advance towards better forms of life and freedom. Christians are present within this movement: important sections of the hierarchy (bishops, priests, ministers), of the base Christian communities, the pastoral organizations concerned with social affairs (land, indigenous peoples, slum-dwellers, marginalized women, young people, the handicapped, human rights, Bible circles, health groups, etc.), who ask themselves, 'How can we at the same time satisfy the people's hunger for God and their hunger for bread? How can we ensure that the gospel is not just a promise of eternal life, but also a force to enable us to attain here a dignified human life on earth as a result of the social transformation brought about by the oppressed themselves, those primarily interested in any social liberation?' In all the spaces listed above, the new evangelization is taking place in the way Puebla described: dynamic, that is, not the mere repetition of things said and taught in the past, but flexible and alive, showing the humanizing potential of the gospel; attractive, that is, structured in a form appropriate to the outlook of the impoverished and uneducated masses; and finally convincing, in other words, generating a new meaning for life by condemning the forms of historic oppression which still remain on the continent and promoting a commitment to liberation which helps in the building of a society which is more participatory and life-enhancing.

Here are some of the features which make this evangelization new.

1. It is new because its primary agents are the poor themselves. They evangelize other poor people and the whole church, especially bishops and priests, who are brought to make an option of solidarity with the poor and marginalized.

2. It is new because it is based more on the gospel than on church doctrine formalized in catechisms. The gospel is read communally in the groups, interpreted in an environment of prayer and ecclesial communion and lived in confrontation with the world of the poor, marked by oppression.

3. It is new because of the new audience, the culture of the people, the oppressed, blacks, marginalized women, abandoned children (about 23 million in Brazil alone), the landless and the homeless, the slum-dwellers; never in the history of Latin America have the oppressed been so central in theology and pastoral work.

4. It is new because it uses new methods based on those made famous by Paulo Freire in such terms as 'the pedagogy of the oppressed' and 'education as the practice of liberation'. In these methods catechumen and catechist enter a process of mutual learning of the faith based on an exchange of experiences which are recognized, criticized and developed in a global perspective, which takes into account the various dimensions of human experience: personal, social, affective, religious and cultural.

5. It is new because it expresses new ideas deriving from the engagement of faith with social injustice. There is an emphasis on the tenet of revelation which is so relevant to the situation of Latin America, the essential connection between the God of life, the cry of the poor and liberation, the relationship between the kingdom of God which is beginning to establish itself through the poor and the successful conclusion of history, always bearing in mind the dialectic of the anti-kingdom, which also takes historical form and produces martyrs, abuse of the name of God and attacks on human life.

6. It is new because it is inaugurating a new way of being church characterized by community, by the involvement of all, by a distribution of functions, by the emergence of new ministries and charisms, by the new type of Christian, involved in the fate of society, in solidarity with the poorest and committed to major changes in society for the benefit of the oppressed.

7. It is new because it produces a new spirituality manifested in the community's daily life, in the celebrations which, in addition to the mysteries of faith, talk about the community's struggles and joys, in the political holiness which is taking shape through involvement in community causes which often imply persecution and even martyrdom – the Latin American church today is a church of martyrs.

8. It is new lastly because it is creating a new relationship between the church and the world, abandoning the alliance with the powerful and joining with the oppressed sectors, defending their rights and showing that Christianity is not a prisoner of the capitalist system, but can be a powerful force for social mobilization to achieve a new society which is more open and participatory.

II. Challenges which renew evangelization

I should now like briefly to touch on the challenges which the Latin

American churches are facing, since it is in these areas that the new evangelization is being worked out.

(a) The evangelization of cultures
In first place is the problem of Latin American cultures. It is an extremely complex situation, because it is the scene of tension and conflict between the indigenous peoples, a majority in a number of countries, people of mixed race, black people, those transplanted by immigration, and currently the newly emerging peoples, the product of the whole historical process among the currently existing nationalities. We know that the arrival of the Spanish and Portuguese produced not a meeting, but a clash of cultures, a relationship of domination and destruction. The Pontifical Commission for Justice and Peace's document *The Church and Racism* (1989) recognizes the facts with precision:

> The first great wave of European colonization was indeed accompanied by a massive destruction of the pre-Colombian civilizations and a brutal subjugation of their populations . . . Soldiers and traders killed to establish themselves; in order to profit from the labour of the indigenous population and, later, of the blacks, they reduced them to slavery (3).

The idea of evangelizing cultures in Latin America only makes sense in relation to this trauma, and therefore from a perspective of liberation, that is, starting from the restoration, recognition and promotion of the cultures of the dominated. This applies in the first place to the witness-cultures of the indigenous peoples. It constitutes a huge challenge, to discover paths by which the indigenous can have access to the Christian message, disentangled from the cultural and denominational interests in which it has always been presented. For important segments of the church the new evangelization means a radical option, profound respect for the culture of each indigenous nation, including its religion, and encouraging its development. These parts of the church support indigenous organization for autonomy, and encourage any means which will restore their birth rate. It is genuine good news (gospel) for the cultures of the Inca, the Maya, the Quechua, the Xavante, the Tupi-Guarani and the others who were historically dominated to know that they can count on the support of broad parts of the church in order to preserve their cultural and religious identity. Obviously the churches are attempting to improve the type of institutional presence they first established 500 years ago, but they cannot shake off the stigma of the conquest of souls which took place in association with the colonial enterprise of the conquest of bodies. The gospel of solidarity with the indigenous peoples creates the minimum conditions for the gospel of liberation. The five centuries of indigenous resistance must not remain in vain: the churches are accepting their share of responsibility for making this unspeakable suffering an element in the formation of the people of God of Amerindia, which must involve the re-establishment of the people.

Black people are a particular challenge. The churches owe them a debt of justice, becauase institutionally they were closer to the estate houses than to the slave-quarters. Large groups within the churches are recognizing the originality of black culture and the legitimacy of their religions, and are accepting the process of syncretism which they have established over the years, as a form of resistance and inculturation of Christianity within the narrow limits of slavery. The value they give to the body, to dance, to the sacramental character of material elements, can enormously enrich Christian experience.

Popular culture has created its religious expression; it does not mean the decadence of official Christianity, but is the way in which the oppressed people assimilated, in their symbolic categories, the Christian message. Today, with very many Christians active in the ecclesial base communities, in trade unions, in popular movements, in the politics which is searching for an alternative to the current forms of domination, a new type of Christianity is appearing, with its own reflection (the source of the theology of liberation), its celebrations, its songs, its historical references, its martyrs and its capacity for mobilization. This type of Christianity is recovering the social, political, libertarian and eschatological dimensions of the gospel. Liberation is not a category which evaporates in spiritualism, but points forward to a process by which the oppressed gradually organize and open spaces of social freedom. To those who believe, these achievements are part of the fullness of the kingdom of God.

(b) Evangelization and economic challenges

Latin America is struggling with a serious economic crisis, of which the foreign debt is only the most visible expression. This fact directly affects evangelization, because it brings on to the scene the huge reality of the poor. They make up the great majority of the population all over the continent. Since the 1960s the Latin American churches have developed a carefully thought-out pastoral policy to face this challenge. They have abandoned assistentialism, charity which encouraged no participation on the part of the recipients, and adopted the preferential option for the poor, which is today the trademark of the Latin American pastoral approach. The option for the poor means a belief in the historical power of the poor and is an attempt to replace poverty through the involvement of the poor themselves in changing their conditions, in their communities, by involvement in trade unions, in political parties rooted in the mass of the people and with a libertarian approach. The poor are only freed from the oppression of poverty when they themselves are the agents of their liberation. The sectors of the church committed to liberation insist on the challenge posed to evangelization by the real poor, the economically poor, in distinction from groups on the whole remote from the hardships of the people which prefer to talk about evangelical poverty. It is true that the term 'evangelical poverty' refers to others besides the economically poor, but it cannot be used to dilute the scandal of material poverty, because this directly affects the biological substance of the poor. If we do not attack this type of poverty in the name of the gospel of Jesus, as a challenge to evangelization, we will be mocking the real poor by giving them a version of religion as in fact opium, a religion cynical in the face of the cry of millions of oppressed. It is no accident that James, Cephas and John, the pillars of the primitive Christian community, after confirming the orthodoxy of Paul's gospel, stipulated that he should show concern for the poor, something the apostle 'was anxious to do in any case' (cf. Gal. 2.10), from the beginning of his missionary work. The evangelization of the poor through and with the poor themselves inevitably takes on a political connotation: when they attack the causes of poverty, evangelizers discover the social system which prioritizes capital over labour and exploits workers, and feel the urgent need for a structural transformation of society. In this way aware and critical Christians become agents of social change, inspired by the gospel itself, lived in a context of oppression.

(c) Evangelization and politics

Having been a colony, Latin America is heavily marked by state authoritarianism and violence. Its democracies are all 'guided', strong states supervised by the military to ensure the order required by national and transnational capital. Historically the churches were accomplices in this situation because they helped to consolidate this form of politics. However, in the last thirty years, as a result of their growing insertion in the world of the poor, most of the churches have turned into spaces of freedom, critical awareness opposed to abuses of power, and sources of condemnation of human rights violations. Ecclesial base communities provide practice in the democratic exercise of power, and in mass-based pastoral work there is a deliberate effort to stimulate participation from the bottom up. There are political parties who rely on the active presence of these new Christians to take into the political arena respect for ordinary people, the vision of social change in accordance with the hopes of the oppressed, and a sense of the value of human subjectivity and moral and religious ideals. Popular culture, including black and indigenous culture, encourages forms of social structure which point towards democratic and participatory socialism. This evangelization is whole, since it does not deal only with typically religious issues; without reducing itself to politics, it engages with politics, enabling politics to be seen as one of the principal areas in which the blessings of the kingdom are made real, to the extent that it is a means of organizing the common quest for the common good.

(d) Evangelization and the world of symbol

Christianity was the religion of the whites, of the invaders, the dominant. Despite this it penetrated deeply into the culture both of the élites and of the masses. At the official level, Latin American Christianity produced no innovations in relation to European Christianity; it simply reproduces it. However, at the popular level Christianity acquired distinctive features; perhaps it is the most important cultural creation on the continent, made possible because it escaped the social and religious controls which affected the other Christianity. The ordinary people were able to create their feasts, express their vision of God, Christ, the Spirit and the saints, their understanding of nature and human destiny. The so-called church of the poor, made up of the vast network of Christian communities and popular movements influenced by them (the land movement, blacks, indigenous, women, etc.), provides the space in which popular culture can express itself. One of the most beautiful and convincing features of the church of the poor is the way ordinary people participate in the commentary on the word of God, the way celebrations are organized, the importance in them of rhythm, dance, and bodily expression, the way in which the people, influenced by the African and indigenous traditions, organize communal work, the meaning they give to death, and the depth of religious experience. It cannot be denied that a new face of Christianity is appearing in Latin America, typical of the fusion of races and cultures, synthesized through popular culture.

(e) Evangelization and ecclesiogenesis

The penetration of the gospel into popular culture has made possible the beginning of a genuine ecclesiogenesis, that is, the genesis of a church born of the faith of the people. Human groups, poor and Christian, which were previously neglected by the ecclesiastical organization (pastoral organizations and parishes) are now beginning to come together around the reading of the word of God, read, that is, against the background of real-life problems. This is the origin of ecclesial base communities. Connected with each other, and with the presence of priests, religious and bishops who take part in their journey, they form the popular church, the church of the poor, with a particular style of living the faith, distributing sacral power among their members, organizing the celebrations of the sacraments and the struggles of the community. This model of the church makes it possible for women to exercise leadership, and is not felt as a break but as in communion with the model of the church which has come from the tradition and persists down to today. We cannot say what will be the future of this type of communitarian Christianity, but it represents the expression of Christianity appropriate to the new culture emerging on the continent, a Christianity which is ecumenical, democratic, militant in the struggle for a new society, incorporates the feminine dimension and is in communion with other historical forms of Christianity.

(f) Evangelization and the process of personalization

Evangelization always holds out a personal utopia, the vision of the new man and the new woman. The new evangelization which is taking place in Latin America is an attempt to achieve a new integration of the human person around the values of participation, freedom, creativity, conviviality open in all directions, all possibilities historically denied to the great majority of the population. These personal values are built on solidarity and in communion with the struggles of the oppressed who are denied the possibility of personhood. Because of this, individual liberation only retains its human and gospel stature if it is able to engage with social liberation. In the communities there is an insistence that the new life should be lived here and now, of course only in germ but nonetheless genuinely; otherwise the old model will dominate and liberation will continue to be a mere utopia without its historical anticipations.

(g) Evangelization and pedagogy

How do we ensure that evangelization is really liberating? This is a constant concern in the church of the poor. The challenge is educational. The missionaries always had this concern. They would learn the languages of the indigenous peoples; they would use theatre and music to impart the elements of the Christian message. But there was never a process of dialogue with the religion of the indigenous peoples or the blacks; instead they were considered works of the devil, to be destroyed. Education served exclusively for the transmission of doctrine – a Roman Catholic circumcision for indigenous peoples and blacks – and not to produce a synthesis from the meeting of cultures. This explains the constant complaint of the missionaries that they learned little or nothing. Education was training in Iberian culture. Today there is a growing awareness that education must be liberating in the sense of involving evangelizer and evangelized, recognizing the presence of the Word and his Spirit in different cultures, accepting differences as legitimate, and being prepared to learn from each other in the context of the same mission of service to the world and the sub-world (the gospel redeems humanity by starting with the victims).

An attractive example of this education for liberation through insertion in the alien culture is available at the very beginnings of evangelization in Latin America, the apparition of the Virgin of Guadelupe to the Aztec Indian Juan Diego in 1531. Mary adapts totally to the cultural world of the Aztecs: she doesn't speak Spanish but Nauhatl; uses Aztec theological language ('the most true God, through whom there is life, the Lord of the near and immediate'); expresses herself in the significant symbols and colours of indigenous culture (her clothes, the sun, the moon, the stars, the angels); appears, not as Spanish, but as a woman of mixed race, on the mountain (Tepeyac) where the Aztecs already worshipped the 'venerable Mother'. The church could only see the miraculous character of the event, not its form, the language, the relationship implied between centre and periphery, the symbolic function of Uncle Juan Bernardino: that is, the educational and evangelizing significance of the event. The current new evangelization attempts to prolong the intuitions present in Guadelupe – the most popular devotion in Latin America – and develop an evangelization which penetrates the cultural structures of the peoples of Latin America.

(h) Evangelization and the safeguarding of the sacred gift of life
The first effect of liberation is to produce life for all and liberation for the poor. This is the essential aim of the new Latin American evangelization. It has helped us to understand that today this cannot be reduced to liberation understood simply in terms of Latin America. The whole earth is threatened. As a result, the basic question is not how far cultures and peoples are evangelized, but how far the gospel and the churches who regard themselves as the historic bearers of the gospel help to save life and all ecosystems from total destruction. Paraphrasing Bartolomé de las Casas, we may say: 'We prefer a human race pagan but alive to a human race Christian but dead, because God is a living God whose glory lies in seeing human beings alive.' In any part of the world, to take up the cause of life, of the means of life, to help to develop a full ecological consciousness, one of respect, love and protection for every type of life (everything that lives deserves to live), is already to carry out the basic intention of the gospel of the one who said, 'I have come that they may have life, life to the full' (John 10.10).

III. The new evangelization and the rediscovery of theology

Doing evangelization from a people's, liberationist, perspective has encouraged the rediscovery of fundamental theological themes. So, for example, Latin American theology has explored the idea of God as the God of life, who takes sides with all those who cry out for life and reveals himself as the liberator of the oppressed. The experience of the church as a network of communities has made it easier to understand the true concept of the Christian God as a God who is a communion of divine persons. The true nature of God is the communion (*koinonia*) between the Father, Son and Holy Spirit which radiates out into creation and history and finds its reflection in Christian communities, which have often proclaimed in their meetings, 'The Blessed Trinity is the perfect community.' The practice of evangelization has made us discover the practice of Jesus as something which produces gospel, that is, good news, in so far as the poor were given priority, the sick cured, the sinners forgiven and the dead raised. It is through the poor and the victims of discrimination that we discover the historical meaning of the kingdom of God which is beginning to be established in the transformation of their situation. If we do not proclaim Jesus as liberator, we will not be being faithful to the tradition of the evangelists and apostles. The church of the poor has discovered the Holy Spirit as a force of cohesion in the community, as enthusiasm and happiness in work, as courage to face the powerful, as consolation for the many who despair because of poverty, as the intelligence which appears in the commentaries of the people of God on the words of the gospel, extracting new meanings which bring the message of Jesus up to date in the contexts in which they live and suffer. The new evangelization has made it possible to build a church as an active community, meeting to celebrate faith and life, organize witness in society as service to life and liberation. Finally, the new evangelization gives new importance to the gospel utopia of a reconciled world of brothers and sisters, but one already starting now to the extent that relationships are built which ensure genuine human society in justice and solidarity.

In conclusion, the new evangelization which is under way in Latin America does justice to the oppressed, the indigenous peoples, blacks, half-castes, women and the poor, who today have the opportunity to hear a complete gospel, and not one mutilated by the interests of colonial power. This gospel does not merely promise them life and freedom; it has become a historical force through the poor as they organize in their communities, able to produce, in alliance with other forces, life and freedom here and now. This is the continuing mission of Jesus, the force of his Spirit made present in this process. Are these not the works which the Father wants to see performed by his sons and daughters in Latin America?

Translated by Francis McDonagh

The New Humanity of the Americas

Virgil Elizondo

1992 calls not for a celebration but for a new creation! It calls not for breast-beating but for deliverance. It calls not for historical continuity but for rupture – a cutting of the umbilical cord from mother Europe and Western civilization. The time has come for the spiritual declaration of independence of the Americas.

The only way to go beyond simplistic condemnation or arrogant triumphalism is to transcend categories of defeat or victory and see the beginning of the Americas for what it truly was: the long and painful birth of the new human person – a new human individual, community, civilization, religion and race. Anthropologically speaking, five hundred years is a very brief period in the birth of a race, and that is precisely what we are witnessing in the Americas.

Nothing as painful, as far-reaching and as fascinating has happened in the history of humanity since the birth of the European some 35,000 years ago, when the Cro-magnons migrated, conquered, massacred the native Neanderthals and mated with them to produce the basis of today's European peoples. The only similar event in world history is the arrival of the Iberians in the Americas which marked the beginning of the new American race – the Mestizo! A new genetic and cultural group was born. It would take centuries to develop. But a new race had been born.[1]

The greatest undiscovered wealth of the Americas is the rich genetic pool – cultural, religious and biological – which constitutes the Americas. We must rediscover not only our great European past but equally the rich heritage of our native ancestors: Quetzalcoatl, Nezahualcoyotl and many others. We truly have the opportunity to create a new humanity like the world has never known. It will not be easy, but it can and must be done if America[2] is to survive. The long, scandalous and painful process of the past five hundred years has been well brought out by the previous authors of this issue. Now, we must dream and work creatively for a new beginning. Out of the crucified peoples of the Americas of yesterday and today, a new humanity will resurrect. We have no doubt of this. The God of life will triumph over the forces of death.

It has taken Europe many centuries and generations of progress and upheavals; of wars and agreements of peace; of crisis, confusion and new synthesis; of universalization and regionalization. Their rich Greco-Roman-Gothic past has constantly been rediscovered, reinterpreted and synthesized with the new ideas of the day to announce new and more exciting possibilities for the human spirit.[3] Finally, in 1992, Europe is coming together to work as a united Europe. Not necessarily a uniform Europe, but definitely a united Europe for the good of all its peoples. The new age of continents has arrived. A new Europe will be born – but will a new humanity be born in Europe? There seem to be no signs of this at the present moment.

We in the Americas are very young! We cannot wait 2000 years to come together as a united America for the good of all Americans – from the tip of Argentina to the upper tip of Newfoundland. The growing inner failure of the USA/American dream of a good life for all coupled with the massive increase of impoverished, undernourished and medically un-cared-for peoples throughout the Americas demands nothing less than a radical and creative new beginning.

The creative dreams that will transform reality from battlefields to farmlands, from opulence at the cost of starvation of others to a new human family of concerned neighbours, from corruption of the mighty to a spirit of authority for the sake of service, from individualism to a sense that it is only within a healthy community that healthy individuals will arise and flourish, and from a sense of nationalism to a sense of continental identity and solidarity, will not come from those whose present-day wealth and security come from the culture and socio-economic structures of today's world. They will struggle and fight to maintain the *status quo*. The creative dreams can only come from where they have always come: the prophetic cries and the utopian imagination of the victims of today's materialistic world.[4]

Out of crisis, suffering and misery, the prophets of old dared to proclaim a new heaven and a new earth. Today, it is the crucified peoples of the Americas that will come forth with the utopian dream of the new and truly universal (inclusive of all) humanity of the Americas. The great paradox, as Jon Sobrino brings out, is that those whose body and blood the dominant society has taken in order to enrich itself,[5] will now become the instruments of the new life of the Americas. It is they who will become God's agents in bringing in the new humanity. It is the Juan Diegos[6] of today who will bring hope to the hopeless and salvation to those who are perishing in their materialistic securities without even knowing it.

Our challenge for 1992 is to begin building the New America – the new humanity which will be something really new in the midst of this world ripped apart by wars, materialism, power-games, consumerism, racism and the like. The challenge: how to get started? Why not convoke the first Ecumenical Council of the Americas?

As our ancient foundational stories about the origins of life in these lands tell us how in the very beginning the gods took council at Teotihuacan so as to give birth to men and women, why not convoke a new Council at Teotihuacan to search for the new humanity of the Americas? This would be an inspired way to make a true beginning in 1992.

Such a Council should involve representatives of all the leading religions and churches of the Americas. It should also involve men and women who truly represent the exploited, excluded and suffering peoples of the Americas. The fundamental credentials for participating in such a Council would be the personal acceptance that much of our Western American civilization is failing humanity, that more patchwork will not help, that the signs of decay and the end are more and more in sight, and that a radical new beginning is the only way to guarantee life into the next millennium. The models cannot be provided by those in the dominant groups, for they are too attached to their securities to be able to think clearly.

Those coming together would assemble – perhaps in a tent city – at Teotihuacan, the ancient city of the gods, to fast, pray and abstain together so as to be open to the great Spirit of God rather than defenders of petty interests. As Moses went into the desert for a new beginning, as Jesus went into the desert truly to discern the will of God and had to struggle against the temptations of the average good person of this world, so too would the members of this religious assembly of the Americas go into the desert to discover God's way.

We could repent together for our sins of the past, give thanks for the blessings of the past and begin to forge a new future together. Out of the best of the roots of our past traditions – the ancient nations of this land, the Iberian world, the Anglo-Saxon world, the African world – a truly new American synthesis could begin to be worked out. Our native ancestors saw the earth as the sacred living entity which constantly gave birth to new life. Our European ancestors saw the God of heaven as the author of life and, in the name of the Lord of heaven, proceeded to possess and destroy Mother Earth. Today the sacredness and unity of heaven and earth can be celebrated in the new life of the Americas. Without question, today's America has not only impoverished the original native peoples of this world by robbing them of their lands, their cultures, their religion and their humanity, but it has impoverished itself by ridiculing their beliefs and ignoring and destroying their values! Isn't it amazing how through the failure of our Western American civilization in relation to questions of the environment, we are today discovering the great truth and wisdom of the sacredness of Mother Earth as lived and proclaimed by our ancient ancestor of this land?

This Council would not be called to discuss church questions or dogmas such as the nature of God, revelation, priesthood, sacraments, episcopacy, but to search out from within the most sacred and ancient traditions of each what is the image of the human which we should be living and promoting. The truth of God leads us to the truth about man and woman. It is not a question of relativizing the sacred doctrines of any one group but rather seeking what we have in common in favour of the human family.

Nor will this Council come together simplistically to condemn Western civilization as such. Throughout its centuries of struggle Western civilization has made great contributions in favour of the human family: the quest for learning, the development of the arts, science, technology, the quest for freedom and justice. The human and humanizing aspects of life that Western civilization has been accumulating across the centuries are great treasures. But the materialistic and individualistic extremes to which Western civilization has gone are threatening to destroy it from within at the same time that it is destroying the weak and poor of this world – almost consuming and feeding upon their bodies and blood in order to satisfy its apparently unsatiable appetite.

Furthermore it will not be a matter of simply listening to the problems of the poor and suffering of the Americas and trying to solve them according to the Western models of becoming human. Much more than that, it will be asking them to share with the rest of the Americas the very humanizing values which, in spite of their marginalization, they have managed to keep alive and pass on from generation to generation. Salvation and new creation always come out of God's poor.

What a world-shaking event it will be! Here the Quechuas, the Aymaras, the Tetzalos, the Mayas, the Navajos, Quiches, the Yaquis, the Tarahumnaras, the Protestants, the Catholics, the Orthodox, the Muslims, the Jews – all the religions which live in this land – will come together in the most ancient sacred site of the Americas, geographically in the very centre of the Americas, to take counsel and listen to the divine spirit at work in us. Coming together not to argue about God, but precisely because we believe in the God who is the creator of men and women, to seek ways of truly bringing new human life into the Americas God has entrusted unto us. What an incredible wealth of religious knowledge in favour of men and women coming to the fullness of life! What a tribute to the creator that we in the Americas could become fully alive! This would be more than a celebration; it would be a marvellous manifestation of the glory of God.

The Ecumenical Council of the Americas will be a far greater event than the arrival of Columbus 1492. It will truly be a first in world history – various religions coming together for the sake of men and women. Respecting each others' sacred doctrines and traditions, but praying, dreaming and working together for the sake of humanity. What a power it will be if all the religions and all the churches, each respecting their own doctrines and dogmas, can agree on the fundamental principles of what it means to be truly human, of what it will take to build up the new family of the Americas, of what are the vices that must be struggled against and the virtues that must be promoted to truly build up the human family.

'In my Father's house there are many mansions.' Can you imagine the great gift the Americas will be to the world if the great religions, rather than ignoring or fighting one another, find ways of working together for the common good? The Pope and the leaders of the great religions of the world prayed together at Assisi; why can we not go even beyond this in the Americas? No one needs to surrender, but each one can work for the good of all. All will be enriched, and the God who is beyond all human expression will be glorified.

A new family of the Americas! If Europe can be a united family by 1992, why cannot the Americas be one? No more national borders separating us one from the other. People will easily, and at will, travel throughout the Americas. What a cause for celebration – no more 'illegals' in the land. America will finally be the common home of all its peoples. Efforts and monies for military defence will be re-routed for affordable housing, education, medicine, agriculture, mass transit, sports and the arts. Land and home ownership will not be reserved to the few who can afford it, but will be available to all the peoples for adequate housing, and there will be plenty of public lands for all to enjoy equally. The goods of the earth will be enjoyed but no longer worshipped. The individual will be important in the context of the primacy of the community, for it is healthy communities that give rise to healthy individuals and not vice versa. There will be rich racial and ethnic diversity, but not discrimination. Men and women in community will be the central focal point of priorities and concerns.

There will be privacy but not isolation, individuality but not individualism, ethnic identity but not ethnocentrism. There will be many religions, but not religious domination, hatred, insult or division. There will be material resources for all, but not misery. It will be a humanity of freedom with responsibility, of humanizing work with leisure time for enjoyment of action and contemplation; of love and sacrifice. Yes, the new humanity of the Americans needs to be conceived and born!

From this Council should come personal commitments and a plan of action, how to bring the 'good news of a new humanity' to the people. We will need the commitment and help of those who today shape the modern mind and heart; the athletes, the song writers and singers, the script-writers, the playwrights, those who produce radio and TV commercials. The preachers, religious educators and teachers all must work together for a new mind-set and new values which will determine our priorities of everyday life.

According to the Mayan scientist/priests who devoted themselves to the mathematical calculations of the ages, the fifth Sun (age) in which we are now living will come to a catastrophic end in the year 2011. Judging by the increase in pollution, weapons and new diseases, and by the general loss of confidence in our present economic, social and religious values, it certainly seems that our present world could easily self-destruct soon.[7] Maybe these predictions are correct. But they will not be the end – they will simply be the end of human imagery and civilizations as we have created them for the benefit of some and the degradation and death of others.

As in the ancient beginning of the Americas, the gods took counsel at Teotihuacan so that the original humanity of today's Americas might be born, today, from this sacred holy ground of the Americas, men and women of God can come together to take counsel so that the new humanity of the Sixth Sun may be born and spread throughout the Americas. The end of our civilization will come. There is no doubt. But there is no fear among the crucified peoples of this land, for they know that in them and through them, new life is already being offered to all the peoples of this land – rich and poor, native, mestizo or immigrant. An age will come to an end, but life will not come to an end. It will be our resurrection – the rebirth of the Americas.

Notes

1. Jacques Ruffie, *De la biologie à la culture*, Paris 1976.
2. Note: whenever I refer to America in this article, I am not limiting it to the USA but use it in reference to the entire American continent – North, Central, South and Caribbean – and hence include all the inhabitants of these lands in the term 'Americans'.
3. Michael Banniard, *Génèse culturelle de l'Europe*, Paris 1989.
4. Ignacio Ellacuría, 'Utopia y profetismo desde America Latina', *Revista Latinoamericana de teologia* 17, 1989.
5. Jon Sobrino, 'How the West was Really Won', in *US Business and World Report*, 21 May 1990.
6. Juan Diego was the low-class Indian to whom Our Lady of Guadalupe appeared

in 1531, asking him to be her messenger. He was the first and foremost evangelizer of the native peoples of Mexico.

7. Frank Waters, *Mexico Mystique: The Coming of Sixth World Consciousness*, Chicago 1975.

Contributors

GUSTAVO GUTIÉRREZ was born in Lima, Peru in 1928. After studying psychology at the University of Louvain and theology at Lyons, he became National Adviser to UNEC (National Union of Catholic Students) and Professor in the Departments of Theology and Social Sciences in the Catholic University of Lima, Peru. His publications include *Le Pastoral de la Iglesia latinoamericana*, Montevideo 1968; *Lineas pastorales de la Iglesia en América Latina* (1970); *Teología de la Liberación* (1971, ET *A Theology of Liberation*, ²1988); *Liberation and Change* (with R. Shaull, 1977); *La Fuerza historica de los pobres* (1979, ET *The Power of the Poor in History*, 1983); *Beber en su proprio pozo* (1983, ET *We Drink from our own Wells*, 1984); *Hablar de Dios*, 1986.

DARCY RIBEIRO, an internationally known anthropologist and a novelist whose novels have been translated into many languages, is one of the leading Brazilian campaigners for indigenous peoples and popular education. He was minister for education and culture, and founder and first rector of the University of Brasília. During his twelve years of exile he planned university reforms in various Latin American countries.

ENRIQUE DUSSEL was born in Argentina in 1934. With a degree in theology and a doctorate in philosophy, he lectures on ethics and Church history in Mexico. He is president of the study commission on Church history of Latin America, and a founder member of the Ecumenical Association of Third World Theologians. He is the author of numerous works on theology and the history of the Church in Latin America, among which the following have recently appeared in English: *Ethics and the Theology of Liberation* (1978); *History of the Church in Latin America, 1492–1980* (1981); *Papers for Liberation Theology* (1981).

AIBAN WAGUA was born in 1944 in Ogobskun, a Kuna Indian (Panama). He gained his doctorate in Education Sciences at the Salesian Pontifical

University in Rome. Since 1981 he has been working with his Kuna people in the community of Ustupu, Kuna Yala. He is a member of the International Commission for his Kuna community, as well as being responsible for reforms and studies for laws obtaining between the State of Panama and the Kuna Yala Province. He has various published works, including indigenous poems and essays. He has taken part in many indigenous congresses, meetings and seminars, some at international level. He has been a priest since 1975, ordained by Pope Paul VI.

PABLO RICHARD was born in Chile in 1939, gained a degree in theology in 1966 from the Catholic University of Chile, a licenciate in sacred scripture in 1969 from the Pontifical Biblical Institute in Rome, and a doctorate in the sociology of religion in 1978 from the Sorbonne in Paris. At present he lives in Costa Rica, where he is titular professor of theology in the national university and a member of DEI (Departamento Ecuménico de Investigaciones), devoted to the continuing formation of pastoral workers from base communities among the poor in Central America. His most recent books are: *La Iglesia latinoamericana entre el temor y la esperanza,* San José ⁴1987; *Death of Christendoms, Birth of the Church,* Maryknoll 1988; *La Fuerza Espiritual de la Iglesia de los Pobres,* San José 1987.

JULIA ESQUIVEL is Guatemalan and a teacher. She studied pastoral theology in the Latin American Bible Seminary in Costa Rica and in the Institut Oecuménique in Bossey in Switzerland. She has published three books of poems.

JOSÉ OSCAR BEOZZO was born in Santa Adélia, São Paulo, Brazil, in 1941, and ordained priest in the diocese of Lins 1964. He studied philosophy in São Paulo, theology at the Gregorian University in Rome, and sociology and social communication at the University of Louvain. He is executive secretary of CESEP (Ecumenical Centre for Services to Evangelization and Popular Education) in São Paulo, a member of the managing committee of CEHILA (Commission for the Study of the History of the Church in Latin America), professor in the faculty of theology in São Paulo and parish priest in Lins. He is a member of the editorial committee of the Theology and Liberation series. He edited volume II/2 of the CEHILA series *História da Igreja na América Latina,* and is the author of various books, including *Materiales para una Historia de la Teologia en América Latina* (1981) and *... E o branco chegou com a espada e a cruz* (1987).

LAËNNEC HURBON was born in Haiti in 1940; he gained his doctorate in theology at the Institut Catholique in Paris and in sociology at the Sorbonne, and is now director of the National Centre of Scientific Research in France; he is also Director of the Haitian/Caribbean journal *Chemins critiques*, published in Haiti. His publications include *Dieu dans le vaudou haitien*, Paris 1972: *Ernst Bloch: Utopie et Espérance*, Paris 1974; *Culture et dictature en Haiti. L'imaginaire sans contrôle*, Paris 1979; *Comprendre Haiti, Essai sur l'Etat, la nation, la culture*, Paris 1987; and *Le Barbare imaginaire*, Paris 1988; he has also edited *Le phénomene religieux dans la Caraibe*, Montreal and Paris 1990.

MAXIMILIANO SALINAS was born in Santiago de Chile in 1952. He is a layman, gained a first degree in theology at the Catholic University of Chile in 1976, and in 1985 defended his doctoral thesis in theology at the Pontifical University of Salamanca. He did research in the faculty of theology of Santiago de Chile from 1976 to 1982. In 1976 he helped to set up the Vicariate of Solidarity in Chile. He is the co-ordinator of the project on the history of Latin American theology within CEHILA (the Commission for the History of the Church in Latin America), and since 1986 has been a member of the Chilean Popular Pastoral Theology Service Team (ESTEPA). His publications include: *Hacia una teología de los pobres*, Lima 1980; *Clotario Blest, profeta de Dios contra el capitalismo*, Santiago 1987; and *Historia del pueblo de Dios en Chile. La evolución del christianismo desde la perspectiva de los pobres*, Santiago 1987.

JOHANN-BAPTIST METZ was born in 1928 in Auerbach (Bavaria), was ordained priest in 1954, holds doctorates in philosophy and theology, and is currently Professor of Fundamental Theology in the University of Münster. His publications include: *Armut im Geiste*, 1962; *Christliche Anthropozentrik* 1962; *Zur Theologie der Welt*, 1968 (ET *Theology of the World*, 1969); *Reform und Gegenreformation heute*, 1969; *Kirche im Prozeß der Aufklärung* 1970; *Die Theologie in der interdisziplinären Forschung* 1971; *Leidensgeschichte*, 1973; *Unsere Hoffnung*, 1975; *Zeit der Orden? Zur Mystik und Politik der Nachfolge*, 1977; *Glaube in Geschichte und Gesellschaft*, 1977 (ET *Faith in History and Society*, 1980); *Gott nach Auschwitz*, 1979; *Jenseits bürgerlicher Religion*, 1980; *Unterbrechungen*, 1981; *Die Theologie der Befreiung – Hoffnung oder Gefahr für die Kirche?* 1986; *Zukunftsfähigkeit. Suchbewegungen im Christentum*, 1987; *Lateinamerika und Europa: Dialog der Theologen*, 1988.

JON SOBRINO was born in the Basque country on 27 December 1938. He became a Jesuit in 1956. Since 1957 he has belonged to the Central American Province and usually lives in El Salvador. He was ordained in 1969, having studied philosophy and engineering at St Louis University, and gained his doctorate in theology at Sankt Georgen, Frankfurt, in 1975. His publications include *Cristología desde América Latina*, Mexico ²1976; *Christology at the Crossroads*, Maryknoll and London; *Resurrección de la verdadera Iglesia*, Santander ²1985; *The True Church and the Poor*, Maryknoll and London 1984; *El celibato cristiano en el tercer mundo*, Bogotá 1981); *Oscar Romero*, Lima 1981; *Jesus in Latin America*, Maryknoll 1986: *The Crucified Peoples*, London 1989; *Companions of Jesus. The Murder and Martyrdom of the Salvadorean Jesuits*, London 1990.

LEONARDO BOFF was born in Concórdia, Brazil, in 1938. He was ordained a Franciscan priest in 1964. He studied in Curitiba, Petrópolis and Munich, and is currently Professor of Systematic Theology at the Franciscan Theological Institute in Petrópolis, joint editor of the *Revista Eclesiástica Brasileira*, and editor of the Brazilian edition of *Concilium*. He is also national adviser to the ecclesial base communities. He has published a number of books, including *Jesus Christ Liberator*, 1971; *Church, Charism and Power*, 1981, which brought its author to the dock of the former Holy Office; *E a igreja se fez povo*, 1985; *Trinity, Society, Liberation*, 1987; and *O caminhar da igreja com os oprimidos: do vale de lágrimas a Terra Prometida*, 1988.

VIRGIL ELIZONDO was born in San Antonio, Texas, and studied at the Ateneo University, at the East Asian Pastoral Institute in Manila, and at the Institut Catholique in Paris. Since 1971, he has been president of the Mexican American Cultural Center in San Antonio. He has published numerous books and articles and been on the editorial board of *Concilium*, *Catequesis Latino Americana* and of the *God With Us Catechetical Series*, USA. He does much theological reflection with the grass-roots people in the poor neighbourhoods of the USA.

Members of the Advisory Committee for Theology of the Third World

Directors

Leonardo Boff OFM	Petrópolis RJ	Brazil
Virgil Elizondo	San Antonio, Texas	USA

Members

K. C. Abraham	Bangalore	India
†Duraisamy Amalorpavadass	Mysore	India
Hugo Assmann	Piracicaba	Brazil
Frank Chikane	Braamfontein	South Africa
Zwinglio Mota Dias	Rio de Janeiro RJ	Brazil
Enrique Dussel	Mexico, D.F.	Mexico
Gustavo Gutiérrez	Lima	Peru
François Houtart	Louvain-la-Neuve	Belgium
Joâo Batista Libanio SJ	Belo-Horizonte MG	Brazil
Beatriz Melano Couch	Buenos Aires	Argentina
José Miguez Bonino	Buenos Aires	Argentina
Uriel Molina	Managua	Nicaragua
Ronaldo Muñoz	Santiago	Chile
John Mutiso-Mbinda	Rome	Italy
Alphonse Mgindu Mushete	Kinshasa, Limeta	Zaire
M. A. Odoyoye	Ibadan	Nigeria
Soon-Kyung Park	Seoul	Korea
Juan Hernandez Pico SJ	Mexico, D.F.	Mexico
Aloysius Pieris SJ	Gonawala-Kalaniya	Sri Lanka
Samuel Rayan SJ	Delhi	India
Pablo Richard	San José	Costa Rica
J. Russel Chandran	Bangalore	India
Anselme Titianma Sanon	Bobo-Dioulassa	Upper Volta
Jon Sobrino	San Salvador	El Salvador